POEMS OF R. S. THOMAS

POEMS

—— OF ——

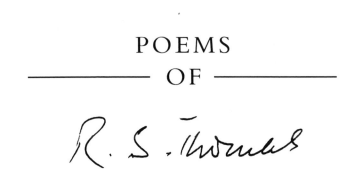

THE UNIVERSITY OF ARKANSAS PRESS

Fayetteville   1985

The University of Arkansas Press, Fayetteville, Ark. 72701
Printed and bound in the United States of America

The University of Arkansas Press gratefully acknowledges the cooperation of Macmillan London, Ltd. and Granada Publishing, Ltd. in the preparation of this collection.

Designer: Patricia Douglas Crowder
Typeface: Linotron 202 Bembo
Typesetter: G&S Typesetters, Inc.
Printer: Thomson-Shore, Inc.
Binder: John H. Dekker & Sons, Inc.

LIBRARY OF CONGRESS CATALOGING IN PUBLICATION DATA

Thomas, R. S. (Ronald Stuart), 1913–
  Poems of R. S. Thomas.

  I. Title.

PR6039.H618A6 1986   821'.914   85-1152
ISBN 0-938626-46-9
ISBN 0-938626-47-7 (pbk.)

CONTENTS

The Way of It (1977)

Frequencies (1978)

Index of Titles

POEMS OF R. S. THOMAS

A PEASANT

Iago Prytherch his name, though, be it allowed,
Just an ordinary man of the bald Welsh hills,
Who pens a few sheep in a gap of cloud.
Docking mangels, chipping the green skin
From the yellow bones with a half-witted grin
Of satisfaction, or churning the crude earth
To a stiff sea of clods that glint in the wind—
So are his days spent, his spittled mirth
Rarer than the sun that cracks the cheeks
Of the gaunt sky perhaps once in a week.
And then at night see him fixed in his chair
Motionless, except when he leans to gob in the fire.
There is something frightening in the vacancy of
       his mind.
His clothes, sour with years of sweat
And animal contact, shock the refined,
But affected, sense with their stark naturalness.
Yet this is your prototype, who, season by sesaon
Against siege of rain and the wind's attrition,
Preserves his stock, an impregnable fortress
Not to be stormed even in death's confusion.
Remember him, then, for he, too, is a winner of wars,
Enduring like a tree under the curious stars.

NIGHT AND MORNING

One night of tempest I arose and went
Along the Menai shore on dreaming bent;
The wind was strong, and savage swung the tide,
And the waves blustered on Caernarfon side.

But on the morrow, when I passed that way,
On Menai shore the hush of heaven lay;

The wind was gentle and the sea a flower,
And the sun slumbered on Caernarfon tower.

(From the Welsh Traditional)

THE CRY OF ELISHA AFTER ELIJAH

The chariot of Israel came,
And the bold, beautiful knights,
To free from his close prison
The friend who was my delight;
Cold is my cry over the vast deep shaken,
Bereft was I, for he was taken.

Through the straight places of Baca
We went with an equal will,
Not knowing who would emerge
First from that gloomy vale;
Cold is my cry; our bond was broken,
Bereft was I, for he was taken.

Where, then, came they to rest,
Those steeds and that car of fire?
My understanding is darkened,
It is no gain to enquire;
Better to await the long night's ending,
Till the light comes, far truths transcending.

I yield, since no wisdom lies
In seeking to go his way;
A man without knowledge am I
Of the quality of his joy;
Yet living souls, a prodigious number,
Bright-faced as dawn, invest God's chamber.

The friends that we loved well,
Though they vanished far from our sight,
In a new country were found
Beyond this vale of night;

O blest are they, without pain or fretting
In the sun's light that knows no setting.

(From the Welsh of Thomas
Williams, Bethesda'r Fro)

SONG FOR GWYDION

When I was a child and the soft flesh was forming
Quietly as snow on the bare boughs of bone,
My father brought me trout from the green river
From whose chill lips the water song had flown.

Dull grew their eyes, the beautiful, blithe garland
Of stipples faded, as light shocked the brain;
They were the first sweet sacrifice I tasted,
A young god, ignorant of the blood's stain.

SONG

Wandering, wandering, hoping to find
The ring of mushrooms with the wet rind,
Cold to the touch, but bright with dew,
A green asylum from time's range.

And finding instead the harsh ways
Of the ruinous wind and the clawed rain;
The storm's hysteria in the bush;
The wild creatures and their pain.

WELSH LANDSCAPE

To live in Wales is to be conscious
At dusk of the spilled blood

That went to the making of the wild sky,
Dyeing the immaculate rivers
In all their courses.
It is to be aware,
Above the noisy tractor
And hum of the machine
Of strife in the strung woods,
Vibrant with sped arrows.
You cannot live in the present,
At least not in Wales.
There is the language for instance,
The soft consonants
Strange to the ear.
There are cries in the dark at night
As owls answer the moon,
And thick ambush of shadows,
Hushed at the fields' corners.
There is no present in Wales,
And no future;
There is only the past,
Brittle with relics,
Wind-bitten towers and castles
With sham ghosts;
Mouldering quarries and mines;
And an impotent people,
Sick with inbreeding,
Worrying the carcase of an old song.

SOIL

A field with tall hedges and a young
Moon in the branches and one star
Declining westward set the scene
Where he works slowly astride the rows
Of red mangolds and green swedes
Plying mechanically his cold blade.

This is his world, the hedge defines
The mind's limits; only the sky
Is boundless, and he never looks up;
His gaze is deep in the dark soil,
As are his feet. The soil is all;
His hands fondle it, and his bones
Are formed out of it with the swedes.
And if sometimes the knife errs,
Burying itself in his shocked flesh,
Then out of the wound the blood seeps home
To the warm soil from which it came.

THE ONE FURROW

When I was young, I went to school
With pencil and foot-rule
Sponge and slate,
And sat on a tall stool
At learning's gate.

When I was older, the gate swung wide;
Clever and keen-eyed
In I pressed,
But found in the mind's pride
No peace, no rest.

Then who was it taught me back to go
To cattle and barrow,
Field and plough;
To keep to the one furrow,
As I do now?

THE MINISTER

Swn y galon fach yn torri

Characters
Narrator   The Minister
Davies   Buddug

The Minister was broadcast on the Welsh Regional
programme of the BBC in 1952.

Narrator

In the hill country at the moor's edge
There is a chapel, religion's outpost
In the untamed land west of the valleys,
The marginal land where flesh meets spirit
Only on Sundays and the days between
Are mortgaged to the grasping soil.

This is the land of green hay
And greener corn, because of the long
Tarrying of winter and the late spring.
This is the land where they burn peat
If there is time for cutting it,
And the weather improves for drying it,
And the cart is not too old for carrying it
And doesn't get stuck in the wet bog.

This is the land where men labour
In silence, and the rusted harrow
Breaks its teeth on the grey stones.
Below, the valleys are an open book,
Bound in sunlight; but the green tale
Told in its pages is not true.

'Beloved, let us love one another,' the words are blown
To pieces by the unchristened wind
In the chapel rafters, and love's text
Is riddled by the inhuman cry
Of buzzards circling above the moor.

Come with me, and we will go
back through the darkness of the vanished years
To peer inside through the low window
Of the chapel vestry, the bare room
That is sour with books and wet clothes.

They chose their pastors as they chose their horses
For hard work. But the last one died
Sooner than they expected; nothing sinister,
You understand, but just the natural
Breaking of the heart beneath a load
Unfit for horses. 'Ay, he's a good 'un,'
Job Davies had said; and Job was a master
Hand at choosing a nag or a pastor.

And Job was right, but he forgot,
They all forgot that even a pastor
Is a man first and a minister after,
Although he wears the sober armour
Of God, and wields the fiery tongue
Of God, and listens to the voice
Of God, the voice no others listen to;
The voice that is the well-kept secret
Of man, like Santa Claus,
Or where baby came from;
The secret waiting to be told
When we are older and can stand the truth.

O, but God is in the throat of a bird;
Ann heard Him speak, and Pantycelyn.
God is in the sound of the white water
Falling at Cynfal. God is in the flowers
Sprung at the foot of Olwen, and Melangell
Felt His heart beating in the wild hare.
Wales in fact is His peculiar home,
Our fathers knew Him. But where is that voice now?
Is it in the chapel vestry, where Davies is using
The logic of the Smithfield?

Davies

A young 'un we want, someone young
Without a wife. Let him learn
His calling first, and choose after
Among our girls, if he must marry.
There's your girl, Pugh; or yours, Parry;
Minister's wives they ought to be
With those white hands that are too soft
For lugging muck or pulling a cow's
Tits. But ay, he must be young.
Remember that mare of yours, John?

Too old when you bought her; the old sinner
Had had a taste of the valleys first
And never took to the rough grass
In the top fields. You could do nothing
With her, but let her go her way.
Lucky you sold her. But you can't sell
Ministers, so we must have a care
In choosing. Take my advice,
Pick someone young, and I'll soon show him
How things is managed in the hills here.

Narrator

Did you notice the farm on the hill side
A bit larger than the others, a bit more hay
In the Dutch barn, four cows instead of two?
Prosperity is a sign of divine favour:
Whoever saw the righteous forsaken
Or his seed begging their bread? It even entitles
A chapel deacon to a tame pastor.

There were people here before these,
Measuring truth according to the moor's
Pitiless commentary and the wind's veto.
Out in the moor there is a bone whitening,
Worn smooth by the long dialectic

Of rain and sunlight. What has that to do
With choosing a minister? Nothing, nothing.

Thick darkness is about us, we cannot see
The future, nor the thin face
Of him whom necessity will bring
To this lean oasis at the moor's rim,
The marginal land where flesh meets spirit
Only on Sundays and the days between
Are mortgaged, mortgaged, mortgaged,
But we can see the faces of the men
Grouped together under the one lamp,
Waiting for the name to be born to them
Out of time's heaving thighs.

Did you dream, wanderer in the night,
Of the ruined house with the one light
Shining; and that you were the moth
Drawn relentlessly out of the dark?
The room was empty, but not for long.
You thought you knew them, but they always changed
To something stranger, if you looked closely
Into their faces. And you wished you hadn't come.
You wished you were back in the wide night
Under the stars. But when you got up to go
There was a hand preventing you.
And when you tried to cry out, the cry got stuck
In your dry throat, and you lay there in travail,
Big with your cry, until the dawn delivered you
And your cry was still-born and you arose and buried it,
Laying on it wreaths of the birds' songs.

But for some there is no dawn, only the light
Of the Cross burning up the long aisle
Of night; and for some there is not even that.

The cow goes round and round the field,
Bored with its grass world, and in its eyes
The mute animal hunger, which you pity,

You the confirmed sentimentalist,
Playing the old anthropomorphic game.
But for the cow, it is the same world over the hedge.
No one ever teased her with pictures of flyless meadows,
Where the grass is eternally green
No matter how often the tongue bruises it,
Or the dung soils it.

But with man it is otherwise.
His slow wound deepens with the years,
And knows no healing only the sharp
Distemper of remembered youth.

The Minister

The Reverend Elias Morgan, B.A.:
I am the name on whom the choice fell.
I came in April, I came young
To the hill chapel, where long hymns were sung
Three times on a Sunday, but rarely between
By a lean-faced people in black clothes,
That smelled of camphor and dried sweat.

It was the time when curlews return
To lay their eggs in the brown heather.
Their piping was the spring's cadenza
After winter's unchanging tune.
But no one heard it, they were too busy
Turning the soil and turning the minister
Over and under with the tongue's blade.

My cheeks were pale and my shoulders bowed
With years of study, but my eyes glowed
With a deep, inner phthisic zeal,
For I was the lamp which the elders chose
To thaw the darkness that had congealed
About the hearts of the hill folk.

I wore a black coat, being fresh from college,
With striped trousers, and, indeed, my knowledge

Would have been complete, had it included
The bare moor, where nature brooded
Over her old, inscrutable secret.
But I didn't even know the names
Of the birds and the flowers by which one gets
A little closer to nature's heart.

Unlike the others my house had a gate
And railings enclosing a tall bush
Of stiff cypress, which the loud thrush
Took as its pulpit early and late.
Its singing troubled my young mind
With strange theories, pagan but sweet,
That made the Book's black letters dance
To a tune John Calvin never heard.
The evening sunlight on the wall
Of my room was a new temptation.
Luther would have thrown his Bible at it.
I closed my eyes, and went on with my sermon.

Narrator

A few flowers bloomed beneath the window,
Set there once by a kind hand
In the old days, a woman's gesture
Of love against the childless years.
Morgan pulled them up; they were untidy.
He sprinkled cinders there instead.

Who is this opening and closing the Book
With a bang, and pointing a finger
Before him in accusation?
Who is this leaning from the wide pulpit
In judgment, and filling the chapel
With sound as God fills the sky?
Is that his shadow on the wall behind?
Shout on, Morgan. You'll be nothing to-morrow.

The people were pleased with their new pastor;
Their noses dripped and the blood ran faster

Along their veins, as the hot sparks
Fell from his lips on their dry thoughts:
The whole chapel was soon ablaze.
Except for the elders, and even they were moved
By the holy tumult, but not extremely.
They knew better than that.

It was sex, sex, sex and money, money,
God's mistake and the devil's creation,
That took the mind of the congregation
On long journeys into the hills
Of a strange land, where sin was the honey
Bright as sunlight in death's hive.
They lost the parable and found the story,
And their glands told them they were still alive.
Job looked at Buddug, and she at him
Over the pews, and they knew they'd risk it
Some evening when the moon was low.

Buddug

I know the place, under the hedge
In the top meadow; it was where my mam
Got into trouble, and only the stars
Were witness of the secret act.
They say her mother was the same.
Well, why not? It's hard on a girl
In these old hills, where youth is short
And boys are scarce; and the ones we'd marry
Are poor or shy. But Job's got money,
And his wife is old. Don't look at me
Like that, Job; I'm trying to listen
To what the minister says. Your eyes
Scare me, yet my bowels ache
With a strange frenzy. This is what
My mother and her mother felt
For the men who took them under the hedge.

Narrator

The moor pressed its face to the window.
The clock ticked on, the sermon continued.
Out in the fir-tree an owl cried
Derision on a God of love.
But no one noticed, and the voice burned on,
Consuming the preacher to a charred wick.

The Minister

I was good that night, I had the *hwyl*.
We sang the verses of the last hymn
Twice. We might have had a revival
If only the organ had kept in time.
But that was the organist's fault.
I went to my house with the light heart
Of one who had made a neat job
Of pruning the branches on the tree
Of good and evil. Llywarch came with me
As far as the gate. Who was the girl
Who smiled at me as she slipped by?

Narrator

There was cheese for supper and cold bacon,
Or an egg if he liked; all of them given
By Job Davies as part of his pay.
Morgan sat down in his white shirt-sleeves
And cut the bacon in slices the way
His mother used to. He sauced each mouthful
With tasty memories of the day.
Supper over, can you picture him there
Slumped in his chair by the red fire
Listening to the clock's sound, shy as a mouse,
Pattering to and fro in the still house?
The fire voice jars; there is no tune to the song
Of the thin wind at the door, and his nearest neighbour

Being three fields' breadth away, it more often seems
That bed is the shortest path to the friendlier morrow.

But he was not unhappy; there were souls to save;
Souls to be rescued from the encroaching wave
Of sin and evil. Morgan stirred the fire
And drove the shadows back into their corners.

The Minister

I held a *seiat*, but no one came.
It was the wrong time, they said, there were the lambs,
And hay to be cut and peat to carry.
Winter was the time for that.
Winter is the time for easing the heart,
For swapping sins and recalling the days
Of summer when the blood was hot.
Ah, the blurred eye and the cold vein
Of age! 'Come home, come home. All is forgiven.'

I began a Bible class;
But no one came,
Only Mali, who was not right in the head.
She had a passion for me, and dreamed of the day. . .
I opened the Bible and expounded the Word
To the flies and spiders, as Francis preached to the birds.

Narrator

Over the moor the round sky
Was ripening, and the sun had spread
Its wings and now was heading south
Over the sea, where Morgan followed.
It was August, the holiday month
For ministers; they walked the smooth
Pavements of Aber and compared their lot
To the white accompaniment of the sea's laughter.

The Minister

When I returned, strengthened, to the bare manse
That smelled of mould, someone had broken a window
During my absence and let a bird in.
I found it dead, starved, on the warm sill.
There is always the thin pane of glass set up between us
And our desires.
We stare and stare and stare, until the night comes
And the glass is superfluous.
I went to my cold bed saddened, but the wind in the tree
Outside soothed me with echoes of the sea.

Narrator

Harvest, harvest! The oats that were too weak
To hold their heads up had been cut down
And placed in stooks. There was no nonsense
Plaiting the last sheaf and wasting time
Throwing sickles. That was fad of Prytherch
Of Nant Carfan; but the bugger was dead.
The men took the corn, the beautiful goddess,
By the long hair and threw her on the ground.

Below in the valleys they were thinking of Christmas;
The fields were all ploughed and the wheat in.
But Davies still hadn't made up his mind
Whom they should ask to the Thanksgiving.

The sea's tan had faded; the old pallor
Was back in Morgan's cheeks. In his long fight
With the bare moor, it was the moor that was winning.
The children came into Sunday School
Before he did, and put muck on his stool.
He stood for the whole lesson, pretending not to notice
The sounds in his desk: a mouse probably
Put there to frighten him. They loved their joke.
Say nothing, say nothing. Morgan was learning
To hold his tongue, the wisdom of the moor.

The pulpit is a kind of block-house
From which to fire the random shot
Of innuendo; but woe betide the man
Who leaves the pulpit for the individual
Assault. He spoke to Davies one day:

Davies

Adultery's a big word, Morgans: where's your proof?
You who never venture from under your roof
Once the night's come; the blinds all down
For fear of the moon's bum rubbing the window.
Take a word from me and keep your nose
In the Black Book, so it won't be tempted
To go sniffing where it's not wanted.
And leave us farmers to look to our own
Business, in case the milk goes sour
From your sharp talk before it's churned
To good butter, if you see what I mean.

Narrator

Did you say something?
Don't be too hard on them, there were people here
Before these and they were no better.
And there'll be people after may be, and they'll be
No better; it is the old earth's way
Of dealing with time's attrition.

Snow on the fields, snow on the heather;
The fox was abroad in the new moon
Barking. And if the snow thawed
And the roads cleared there was an election
Meeting in the vestry next the chapel.
Men came and spoke to them about Wales,
The land they lived in without knowing it,
The land that is reborn at such times.
They mentioned Henry Richard and S. R.—the
    great names;

And Keir Hardie; the names nobody knew.
It was quite exciting, but in the high marginal land
No names last longer than the wind
And the rain let them on the cold tombstone.
They stood outside afterwards and watched the cars
Of the speakers departing down the long road
To civilization, and walked home
Arguing confusedly under the stars.

The Minister

Winter was like that; a meeting, a foxhunt,
And the weekly journey to market to unlearn
The lesson of Sunday. The rain never kept them
From the packed town, though it kept them
        from chapel.

> Drive on, farmer, to market
> With your pigs and your lean cows
> To the town, where the dealers are waiting
> And the girl in the green blouse,
> Fresh as a celandine from the spring meadows,
> Builds like a fabulous tale
> Tower upon tower on the counter
> The brown and the golden ale.

Narrator

A year passed, once more Orion
Unsheathed his sword from its dark scabbard;
And Sirius followed, loud as a bird
Whistling to eastward his bright notes.
The stars are fixed, but the earth journeys
By strange migrations towards the cold
Frosts of autumn from the spring meadows.
And we who see them, where have we been
Since last their splendour inflamed our mind
With huge questions not to be borne?

Morgan was part of the place now; he was beginning
To look back as well as forwards:
Back to the green valleys, forward along the track
That dwindled to nothing in the vast moor.
But life still had its surprises. There was the day
They found old Llywarch dead under the wall
Of the grey sheep-fold, and the sheep all in a ring
Staring, staring at the stiff frame
And the pursed lips from which no whistle came.

The Minister

It was my biggest funeral of all; the hills crawled
With black figures, drawn from remote farms
By death's magnet. 'So sudden. It might have been me.'
And there in the cheap coffin Llywarch was lying,
Taller than you thought, and women were trying
To read through their tears the brass plate.

It might have been Davies! Quickly I brushed
The black thought away; but it came back.
My voice deepened; the people were impressed.
Out in the cold graveyard we sang a hymn,
O fryniau Caersalem; and the Welsh hills looked on
Implacably. It was the old human cry.
But let me be fair, let me be fair.
It was not all like this, even the moor
Has moods of softness when the white hair
Of the bog cotton is a silk bed
For dreams to lie on. There was a day
When young Enid of Gors Fach
Pressed an egg into my hand
Smiling, and her father said:
'Take it, Morgans, to please the child.'
I never heard what they said after,
But went to my bed that night happy for once.
I looked from my top window and saw the moon,
Mellow with age, rising over the moor;
There was something in its bland expression

That softened the moor's harshness, stifled the questions
Struggling to my lips; I made a vow,
As other men in other years have done,
To-morrow would be different. I lay down
And slept quietly. But the morrow woke me
To the ancestral fury of the rain
Spitting and clawing at the pane.
I looked out on a grey world, grey with despair.

Narrator

The rhythm of the seasons: wind and rain,
Dryness and heat, and then the wind again,
Always the wind, and rain that is the sadness
We ascribe to nature, who can feel nothing.
The redwings leave, making way for the swallows;
The swallows depart, the redwings are back once more.
But man remains summer and winter through,
Rooting in vain within his dwindling acre.

The Minister

I was the chapel pastor, the abrupt shadow
Staining the neutral fields, troubling the men
Who grew there with my glib, dutiful praise
Of a fool's world; a man ordained for ever
To pick his way along the grass-strewn wall
Dividing tact from truth.
                    I knew it all,
Although I never pried, I knew it all.
I knew why Buddug was away from chapel.
I knew that Pritchard, the *Fron*, watered his milk.
I knew who put the ferret with the fowls
In Pugh's hen-house. I knew and pretended I didn't.
And they knew that I knew and pretended I didn't.
They listened to me preaching the unique gospel
Of love; but our eyes never met. And outside
The blood of God darkened the evening sky.

Narrator

Is there no passion in Wales? There is none
Except in the racked hearts of men like Morgan,
Condemned to wither and starve in the cramped cell
Of thought their fathers made them.
Protestantism—the adroit castrator
Of art; the bitter negation
Of song and dance and the heart's innocent joy—
You have botched our flesh and left us only the soul's
Terrible impotence in a warm world.

Need we go on? In spite of all
His courage Morgan could not avert
His failure, for he chose to fight
With that which yields to nothing human.
He never listened to the hills'
Music calling to the hushed
Music within; but let his mind
Fester with brooding on the sly
Infirmities of the hill people.
The pus conspired with the old
Infection lurking in his breast.

In the chapel acre there is a grave,
And grass contending with the stone
For mastery of the near horizon,
And on the stone words; but never mind them:
Their formal praise is a vain gesture
Against the moor's encroaching tide.
We will listen instead to the wind's text
Blown through the roof, or the thrush's song
In the thick bush that proved him wrong,
Wrong from the start, for nature's truth
Is primary and her changing seasons
Correct out of a vaster reason
The vague errors of the flesh.

CHILDREN'S SONG

We live in our own world,
A world that is too small
For you to stoop and enter
Even on hands and knees,
The adult subterfuge.
And though you probe and pry
With analytic eye,
And eavesdrop all our talk
With an amused look,
You cannot find the centre
Where we dance, where we play,
Where life is still asleep
Under the closed flower,
Under the smooth shell
Of eggs in the cupped nest
That mock the faded blue
Of your remoter heaven.

THE VILLAGE

Scarcely a street, too few houses
To merit the title; just a way between
The one tavern and the one shop
That leads nowhere and fails at the top
Of the short hill, eaten away
By long erosion of the green tide
Of grass creeping perpetually nearer
This last outpost of time past.

So little happens; the black dog
Cracking his fleas in the hot sun
Is history. Yet the girl who crosses
From door to door moves to a scale
Beyond the bland day's two dimensions.

Stay, then, village, for round you spins
On slow axis a world as vast
And meaningful as any poised
By great Plato's solitary mind.

SONG AT THE YEAR'S TURNING

Shelley dreamed it. Now the dream decays.
The props crumble. The familiar ways
Are stale with tears trodden underfoot.
The heart's flower withers at the root.
Bury it, then, in history's sterile dust.
The slow years shall tame your tawny lust.

Love deceived him; what is there to say
The mind brought you by a better way
To this despair? Lost in the world's wood
You cannot stanch the bright menstrual blood.
The earth sickens; under naked boughs
The frost comes to barb your broken vows.

Is there blessing? Light's peculiar grace
In cold splendour robes this tortured place
For strange marriage. Voices in the wind
Weave a garland where a mortal sinned.
Winter rots you; who is there to blame?
The new grass shall purge you in its flame.

INVASION ON THE FARM

I am Prytherch. Forgive me. I don't know
What you are talking about; your thoughts flow
Too swiftly for me; I cannot dawdle
Along their banks and fish in their quick stream
With crude fingers. I am alone, exposed

In my own fields with no place to run
From your sharp eyes. I, who a moment back
Paddled in the bright grass, the old farm
Warm as a sack about me, feel the cold
Winds of the world blowing. The patched gate
You left open will never be shut again.

TALIESIN 1952

I have been all men known to history,
Wondering at the world and at time passing;
I have seen evil, and the light blessing
Innocent love under a spring sky.

I have been Merlin wandering in the woods
Of a far country, where the winds waken
Unnatural voices, my mind broken
By sudden acquaintance with man's rage.

I have been Glyn Dŵr set in the vast night,
Scanning the stars for the propitious omen,
A leader of men, yet cursed by the crazed women
Mourning their dead under the same stars.

I have been Goronwy, forced from my own land
To taste the bitterness of the salt ocean;
I have known exile and a wild passion
Of longing changing to a cold ache.

King, beggar and fool, I have been all by turns,
Knowing the body's sweetness, the mind's treason;
Taliesin still, I show you a new world, risen,
Stubborn with beauty, out of the heart's need.

JANUARY

The fox drags its wounded belly
Over the snow, the crimson seeds
Of blood burst with a mild explosion,
Soft as excrement, bold as roses.

Over the snow that feels no pity,
Whose white hands can give no healing,
The fox drags its wounded belly.

PISCES

Who said to the trout,
You shall die on Good Friday
To be food for a man
And his pretty lady?

It was I, said God,
Who formed the roses
In the delicate flesh
And the tooth that bruises.

THE RETURN

Coming home was to that:
The white house in the cool grass
Membraned with shadow, the bright stretch
Of stream that was its looking-glass;

And smoke growing above the roof
To a tall tree among whose boughs
The first stars renewed their theme
Of time and death and a man's vows.

A WELSHMAN TO ANY TOURIST

We've nothing vast to offer you, no deserts
Except the waste of thought
Forming from mind erosion;
No canyons where the pterodactyl's wing
Casts a cold shadow.
The hills are fine, of course,
Bearded with water to suggest age
And pocked with caverns,
One being Arthur's dormitory;
He and his knights are the bright ore
That seams our history,
But shame has kept them late in bed.

IN A COUNTRY CHURCH

To one kneeling down no word came,
Only the wind's song, saddening the lips
Of the grave saints, rigid in glass;
Or the dry whisper of unseen wings,
Bats not angels, in the high roof.

Was he balked by silence? He kneeled long,
And saw love in a dark crown
Of thorns blazing, and a winter tree
Golden with fruit of a man's body.

NO THROUGH ROAD

All in vain. I will cease now
My long absorption with the plough,
With the tame and the wild creatures
And man united with the earth.

I have failed after many seasons
To bring truth to birth,
And nature's simple equations
In the mind's precincts do not apply.

But where to turn? Earth endures
After the passing, necessary shame
Of winter, and the old lie
Of green places beckons me still
From the new world, ugly and evil,
That men pry for in truth's name.

EVANS

Evans? Yes, many a time
I came down his bare flight
Of stairs into the gaunt kitchen
With its wood fire, where crickets sang
Accompaniment to the black kettle's
Whine, and so into the cold
Dark to smother in the thick tide
Of night that drifted about the walls
Of his stark farm on the hill ridge.

It was not the dark filling my eyes
And mouth appalled me; not even the drip
Of rain like blood from the one tree
Weather-tortured. It was the dark
Silting the veins of that sick man
I left stranded upon the vast
And lonely shore of his bleak bed.

SAILOR POET

His first ship; his last poem;
And between them what turbulent acres

Of sea or land with always the flesh ebbing
In slow waves over the salt bones.

But don't be too hard; so to have written
Even in smoke on such fierce skies,
Or to have brought one poem safely to harbour
From such horizons is not now to be scorned.

THE CAT AND THE SEA

It is a matter of a black cat
On a bare cliff top in March
Whose eyes anticipate
The gorse petals;

The formal equation of
A domestic purr
With the cold interiors
Of the sea's mirror.

THE LETTER

And to be able to put at the end
Of the letter Athens, Florence—some name
That the spirit recalls from earlier journeys
Through the dark wood, seeking the path
To the bright mansions; cities and towns
Where the soul added depth to its stature.

And not to worry about the date,
The words being timeless, concerned with truth,
Beauty, love, misery even,
Which has its seasons in the long growth
From seed to flesh, flesh to spirit.

And laying aside the pen, dipped
Not in tears' volatile liquid

But in black ink of the heart's well,
To read again what the hand has written
To the many voices' quiet dictation.

THE VIEW FROM THE WINDOW

Like a painting it is set before one,
But less brittle, ageless; these colours
Are renewed daily with variations
Of light and distance that no painter
Achieves or suggests. Then there is movement,
Change, as slowly the cloud bruises
Are healed by sunlight, or snow caps
A black mood; but gold at evening
To cheer the heart. All through history
The great brush has not rested,
Nor the paint dried; yet what eye,
Looking coolly, or, as we now,
Through the tears' lenses, ever saw
This work and it was not finished?

AP HUW'S TESTAMENT

There are four verses to put down
For the four people in my life,
Father, mother, wife

And the one child. Let me begin
With her of the immaculate brow
My wife; she loves me. I know how.

My mother gave me the breast's milk
Generously, but grew mean after,
Envying me my detached laughter.

My father was a passionate man,
Wrecked after leaving the sea
In her love's shallows. He grieves in me.

What shall I say of my boy,
Tall, fair? He is young yet;
Keep his feet free of the world's net.

THE JOURNEY

And if you go up that way, you will meet with a man,
Leading a horse, whose eyes declare:
There is no God. Take no notice.
There will be other roads and other men
With the same creed, whose lips yet utter
Friendlier greeting, men who have learned
To pack a little of the sun's light
In their cold eyes, whose hands are waiting
For your hand. But do not linger.
A smile is payment; the road runs on
With many turnings towards the tall
Tree to which the believer is nailed.

POETRY FOR SUPPER

'Listen, now, verse should be as natural
As the small tuber that feeds on muck
And grows slowly from obtuse soil
To the white flower of immortal beauty.'

'Natural, hell! What was it Chaucer
Said once about the long toil
That goes like blood to the poem's making?
Leave it to nature and the verse sprawls,
Limp as bindweed, if it break at all

Life's iron crust. Man, you must sweat
And rhyme your guts taut, if you'd build
Your verse a ladder.'
                                    'You speak as though
No sunlight ever surprised the mind
Groping on its cloudy path.'

'Sunlight's a thing that needs a window
Before it enter a dark room.
Windows don't happen.'
                                    So two old poets,
Hunched at their beer in the low haze
Of an inn parlour, while the talk ran
Noisily by them, glib with prose.

MEET THE FAMILY

John One takes his place at the table,
He is the first part of the fable;
His eyes are dry as a dead leaf.
Look on him and learn grief.

John Two stands in the door
Dumb; you have seen that face before
Leaning out of the dark past,
Tortured in thought's bitter blast.

John Three is still outside
Drooling where the daylight died
On the wet stones; his hands are crossed
In mourning for a playmate lost.

John All and his lean wife,
Whose forced complicity gave life
To each loathed foetus, stare from the wall,
Dead not absent. The night falls.

THE CURE

But what to do? Doctors in verse
Being scarce now, most poets
Are their own patients, compelled to treat
Themselves first, their complaint being
Peculiar always. Consider, you,
Whose rough hands manipulate
The fine bones of a sick culture,
What areas of that infirm body
Depend solely on a poet's cure.

THE CRY

Don't think it was all hate
That grew there; love grew there, too,
Climbing by small tendrils where
The warmth fell from the eyes' blue

Flame. Don't think even the dirt
And the brute ugliness reigned
Unchallenged. Among the fields
Sometimes the spirit, enchained

So long by the gross flesh, raised
Suddenly there its wild note of praise.

BREAD

Hunger was loneliness, betrayed
By the pitiless candour of the stars'
Talk, in an old byre he prayed

Not for food; to pray was to know
Waking from a dark dream to find
The white loaf on the white snow;

Not for warmth, warmth brought the rain's
Blurring of the essential point
Of ice probing his raw pain.

He prayed for love, love that would share
His rags' secret; rising he broke
Like sun crumbling the gold air

The live bread for the starved folk.

FARM WIFE

Hers is the clean apron, good for fire
Or lamp to embroider, as we talk slowly
In the long kitchen, while the white dough
Turns to pastry in the great oven,
Sweetly and surely as hay making
In a June meadow; hers are the hands,
Humble with milking, but still now
In her wide lap as though they heard
A quiet music, hers being the voice
That coaxes time back to the shadows
In the room's corners. O, hers is all
this strong body, the safe island
Where men may come, sons and lovers,
Daring the cold seas of her eyes.

WALTER LLYWARCH

I am, as you know, Walter Llywarch,
Born in Wales of approved parents,
Well goitred, round in the bum,
Sure prey of the slow virus
Bred in quarries of grey rain.

Born in autumn at the right time
For hearing stories from the cracked lips
Of old folk dreaming of summer,
I piled them on to the bare hearth
Of my own fancy to make a blaze
To warm myself, but achieved only
The smoke's acid that brings the smart
Of false tears into the eyes.

Months of fog, months of drizzle;
Thought wrapped in the grey cocoon
Of race, of place, awaiting the sun's
Coming, but when the sun came,
Touching the hills with a hot hand,
Wings were spread only to fly
Round and round in a cramped cage
Or beat in vain at the sky's window.

School in the week, on Sunday chapel:
Tales of a land fairer than this
Were not so tall, for others had proved it
Without the grave's passport, they sent
The fruit home for ourselves to taste.

Walter Llywarch—the words were a name
On a lost letter that never came
For one who waited in the long queue
Of life that wound through a Welsh valley.
I took instead, as others had done
Before, a wife from the back pews
In chapel, rather to share the rain
Of winter evenings, than to intrude
On her pale body; and yet we lay
For warmth together and laughed to hear
Each new child's cry of despair.

GENEALOGY

I was the dweller in the long cave
Of darkness, lining it with the forms
Of bulls. My hand matured early,

But turned to violence: I was the man
Watching later at the grim ford,
Armed with resentment; the quick stream

Remembers at sunset the raw crime.
The deed pursued me; I was the king
At the church keyhole, who saw death

Loping towards me. From that same hour
I fought for right, with the proud chiefs
Setting my name to the broad treaties.

I marched to Bosworth with the Welsh lords
To victory, but regretted after
The white house at the wood's heart.

I was the stranger in the new town,
Whose purse of tears was soon spent;
I filled it with a solider coin

At the dark sources. I stand now
In the hard light of the brief day
Without roots, but with many branches.

THE FACE

I see his face pressed to the wind's pane,
Staring with cold eyes: a country face
Without beauty, yet with the land's trace
Of sadness, badness, madness. I knew when
I first saw him that was the man
To turn the mind on, letting its beam

Discover rottenness at the seams
Of the light's garment I found him in.

Did I look long enough or too long?
On the weak brow nature's ruthless course
Was charted, but the lips' thin song
Never reached me; rain's decrepit hearse
Carried him off in the slow funeral
Of all his kind, leaving the heart full.

ANNIVERSARY

Nineteen years now
Under the same roof
Eating our bread,
Using the same air;
Sighing, if one sighs,
Meeting the other's
Words with a look
That thaws suspicion.

Nineteen years now
Sharing life's table,
And not to be first
To call the meal long
We balance it thoughtfully
On the tip of the tongue,
Careful to maintain
The strict palate.

Nineteen years now
Keeping simple house,
Opening the door
To friend and stranger;
Opening the womb
Softly to let enter

The one child
With his huge hunger.

JUDGMENT DAY

Yes, that's how I was,
I know that face,
That bony figure
Without grace
Of flesh or limb;
In health happy,
Careless of the claim
Of the world's sick
Or the world's poor;
In pain craven—
Lord, breathe once more
On that sad mirror,
Let me be lost
In mist for ever
Rather than own
Such bleak reflections.
Let me go back
On my two knees
Slowly to undo
The knot of life
That was tied there.

HIRELING

Cars pass him by; he'll never own one.
Men won't believe in him for this.
Let them come into the hills
And meet him wandering a road,
Fenced with rain, as I have now;

The wind feathering his hair;
The sky's ruins, gutted with fire
Of the late sun, smouldering still.

Nothing is his, neither the land
Nor the land's flocks. Hired to live
On hills too lonely, sharing his hearth
With cats and hens, he has lost all
Property but the grey ice
Of a face splintered by life's stone.

POET'S ADDRESS TO THE BUSINESSMEN

Gentlemen all
At the last crumbfall,
The set of glasses,
The moist eye,
I rise to speak
Of things irrelevant:
The poem shut,
Uneasy fossil,
In the mind's rock;
The growth of winter
In the thick wood
Of history; music
We might have heard
In the heart's cloisters.
I speak of wounds
Not dealt us; blows
That left no bruises
On the white table
Cloth. Forgive me
The tongue's failure,
In all this leanness
Of time, to arrive
Nearer the bone.

THOSE OTHERS

A gofid gwerin gyfan
Yn fy nghri fel taerni tân.
                    Dewi Emrys

I have looked long at this land,
Trying to understand
My place in it—why,
With each fertile country
So free of its room,
This was the cramped womb
At last took me in
From the void of unbeing.

Hate takes a long time
To grow in, and mine
Has increased from birth;
Not for the brute earth
That is strong here and clean
And plain in its meaning
As none of the books are
That tell but of the war

Of heart with head, leaving
The wild birds to sing
The best songs; I find
This hate's for my own kind,
For men of the Welsh race
Who brood with dark face
Over their thin navel
To learn what to sell;

Yet not for them all either,
There are still those other
Castaways on a sea
Of grass, who call to me,
Clinging to their doomed farms;
Their hearts though rough are warm
And firm, and their slow wake
Through time bleeds for our sake.

LORE

Job Davies, eighty-five
Winters old, and still alive
After the slow poison
And treachery of the seasons.

Miserable? Kick my arse!
It needs more than the rain's hearse,
Wind-drawn, to pull me off
The great perch of my laugh.

What's living but courage?
Paunch full of hot porridge,
Nerves strengthened with tea,
Peat-black, dawn found me

Mowing where the grass grew,
Bearded with golden dew.
Rhythm of the long scythe
Kept this tall frame lithe.

What to do? Stay green.
Never mind the machine,
Whose fuel is human souls.
Live large, man, and dream small.

MOTHER AND SON

At nine o'clock in the morning
My son said to me:
Mother, he said, from the wet streets
The clouds are removed and the sun walks
Without shoes on the warm pavements.
There are girls biddable at the corners
With teeth cleaner than your white plates;
The sharp clatter of your dishes
Is less pleasant to me than their laughter.
The day is building; before its bright walls

Fall in dust, let me go
Beyond the front garden without you
To find glasses unstained by tears,
To find mirrors that do not reproach
My smooth face; to hear above the town's
Din life roaring in the veins.

A WELSH TESTAMENT

All right, I was Welsh. Does it matter
I spoke the tongue that was passed on
To me in the place I happened to be,
A place huddled between grey walls
Of cloud for at least half the year.
My word for heaven was not yours.
The word for hell had a sharp edge
Put on it by the hand of the wind
Honing, honing with a shrill sound
Day and night. Nothing that Glyn Dŵr
Knew was armour against the rain's
Missiles. What was descent from him?

Even God had a Welsh name:
We spoke to him in the old language;
He was to have a peculiar care
For the Welsh people. History showed us
He was too big to be nailed to the wall
Of a stone chapel, yet still we crammed him
Between the boards of a black book.

Yet men sought us despite this.
My high cheek-bones, my length of skull
Drew them as to a rare portrait
By a dead master. I saw them stare
From their long cars, as I passed knee-deep
In ewes and wethers. I saw them stand
By the thorn hedges, watching me string
The far flocks on a shrill whistle.

And always there was their eyes' strong
Pressure on me: you are Welsh, they said;
Speak to us so; keep your fields free
Of the smell of petrol, the loud roar
Of hot tractors; we must have peace
And quietness.

           Is a museum
Peace? I asked. Am I the keeper
Of the heart's relics, blowing the dust
In my own eyes? I am a man;
I never wanted the drab role
Life assigned me, an actor playing
To the past's audience upon a stage
Of earth and stone; the absurd label
Of birth, of race hanging askew
About my shoulders. I was in prison
Until you came; your voice was a key
Turning in the enormous lock
Of hopelessness. Did the door open
To let me out or yourselves in?

HERE

I am a man now.
Pass your hand over my brow,
You can feel the place where the brains grow.

I am like a tree,
From my top boughs I can see
The footprints that led up to me.

There is blood in my veins
That has run clear of the stain
Contracted in so many loins.

Why, then, are my hands red
With the blood of so many dead?
Is this where I was misled?

Why are my hands this way
That they will not do as I say?
Does no God hear when I pray?

I have nowhere to go.
The swift satellites show
The clock of my whole being is slow.

It is too late to start
For destinations not of the heart.
I must stay here with my hurt.

THE MAKER

So he said then: I will make the poem,
I will make it now. He took pencil,
The mind's cartridge, and blank paper,
And drilled his thoughts to the slow beat

Of the blood's drum; and there it formed
On the white surface and went marching
Onward through time, while the spent cities
And dry hearts smoked in its wake.

THE SURVIVOR

Yesterday I found one left:
Eighty-five, too old for mischief.
What strange grace lends him a brief
Time for repenting of his theft
Of health and comeliness from her
Who lay caught in his strong arms
Night by night and heard the farm's
Noises, the beasts' moan and stir?

The land's thug: seventeen stone,
Settling down in a warm corner

By a wood fire's lazy purr;
A slumped bundle of fat and bone,
Bragging endlessly of his feats
Of strength and skill with the long scythe,
Or gallantry among the blithe
Serving women, all on heat

For him, of course. My mind went back
Sombrely to that rough parish,
Lovely as the eye could wish
In its green clothes, but beaten black
And blue by the deeds of dour men
Too like him, warped inside
And given to watching, sullen-eyed,
Love still-born, as it was then.

Wake him up. It is too late
Now for the blood's foolish dreaming.
The veins clog and the body's spring
Is long past; pride and hate
Are the strong's fodder and the young.
Old and weak, he must chew now
The cud of prayer and be taught how
From hard hearts huge tears are wrung.

FUNERAL

They stand about conversing
In dark clumps, less beautiful than trees.
What have they come here to mourn?
There was a death, yes; but death's brother,
Sin, is of more importance.
Shabbily the teeth gleam,
Sharpening themselves on reputations
That were firm once. On the cheap coffin
The earth falls more cleanly than tears.
What are these red faces for?
This incidence of pious catarrh

At the grave's edge? He has returned
Where he belongs; this is acknowledged
By all but the lonely few
Making amends for the heart's coldness
He had from them, grudging a little
The simple splendour of the wreath
Of words the church lays on him.

SORRY

Dear parents,
I forgive you my life,
Begotten in a drab town,
The intention was good;
Passing the street now,
I see still the remains of sunlight.

It was not the bone buckled;
You gave me enough food
To renew myself.
It was the mind's weight
Kept me bent, as I grew tall.

It was not your fault.
What should have gone on,
Arrow aimed from a tried bow
At a tried target, has turned back,
Wounding itself
With questions you had not asked.

THE GARDEN

It is a gesture against the wild,
The ungovernable sea of grass;
A place to remember love in,

To be lonely for a while;
To forget the voices of children
Calling from a locked room;
To substitute for the care
Of one querulous human
Hundreds of dumb needs.

It is the old kingdom of man.
Answering to their names,
Out of the soil the buds come,
The silent detonations
Of power wielded without sin.

THE UNTAMED

My garden is the wild
    Sea of the grass. Her garden
Shelters between walls.
    The tide could break in;
    I should be sorry for this.

There is peace there of a kind,
    Though not the deep peace
Of wild places. Her care
    For green life has enabled
    The weak things to grow.

Despite my first love,
    I take sometimes her hand,
Following strait paths
    Between flowers, the nostril
    Clogged with their thick scent.

The old softness of lawns
    Persuading the slow foot
Leads to defection; the silence
    Holds with its gloved hand
    The wild hawk of the mind.

But not for long, windows,
  Opening in the trees
Call the mind back
  To its true eyrie; I stoop
  Here only in play.

THE BOY'S TALE

Skipper wouldn't pay him off,
Never married her;
Came home by Port Said
To a Welsh valley;
Took a girl from the tip,
Sheer coal dust
The blue in her veins.
Every time I go now
Through black sunlight,
I see her scratch his name
On the pane of her breath.
Caught him in her thin hair,
Couldn't hold him—
Voices from the ports
Of the stars, pavilions
Of unstable water.
She went fishing in him;
I was the bait
That became cargo,
Shortening his trips,
Waiting on the bone's wharf.
Her tongue ruled the tides.

SOUILLAC: LE SACRIFICE D'ABRAHAM

And he grasps him by the hair
With innocent savagery.
And the son's face is calm;
There is trust there.

And the beast looks on.

This is what art could do,
Interpreting faith
With serene chisel.
The resistant stone
Is quiet as our breath,
And is accepted.

ON THE FARM

There was Dai Puw. He was no good.
They put him in the fields to dock swedes,
And took the knife from him, when he came home
At late evening with a grin
Like the slash of a knife on his face.

There was Llew Puw, and he was no good.
Every evening after the ploughing
With the big tractor he would sit in his chair,
And stare into the tangled fire garden,
Opening his slow lips like a snail.

There was Huw Puw, too. What shall I say?
I have heard him whistling in the hedges
On and on, as though winter
Would never again leave those fields,
And all the trees were deformed.

And lastly there was the girl:
Beauty under some spell of the beast.

Her pale face was the lantern
By which they read in life's dark book
The shrill sentence: God is love.

PIETÀ

Always the same hills
Crowd the horizon,
Remote witnesses
Of the still scene.

And in the foreground
The tall Cross,
Sombre, untenanted,
Aches for the Body
That is back in the cradle
Of a maid's arms.

KIERKEGAARD

And beyond the window Denmark
Waited, but refused to adopt
This family that wore itself out
On its conscience, up and down
In the one room.
                    Meanwhile the acres
Of the imagination grew
Unhindered, though always they paused
At that labourer, the indictment
Of whose gesture was a warped
Crucifix upon a hill
In Jutland. The stern father
Looked at it and a hard tear
Formed, that the child's frightened

Sympathy could not convert
To a plaything.   He lived on,
Søren, with the deed's terrible lightning
About him, as though a bone
Had broken in the adored body
Of his God. The streets emptied
Of their people but for a girl
Already beginning to feel
The iron in her answering his magnet's
Pull. Her hair was to be
The moonlight towards which he leaned
From darkness. The husband stared
Through life's bars, venturing a hand
To pluck her from the shrill fire
Of his genius. The press sharpened
Its rapier; wounded, he crawled
To the monastery of his chaste thought
To offer up his crumpled amen.

RAVENS

It was the time of the election.
The ravens loitered above the hill
In slow circles; they had all air
To themselves. No eyes were lifted
From the streets, no ears heard
Them exulting, recalling their long
History, presidents of the battles
Of flesh, the sly connoisseurs
Of carrion; desultory flags
Of darkness, saddening the sky
At Catraeth and further back,
When two, who should have been friends,
Contended in the innocent light
For the woman in her downpour of hair.

THE MOOR

It was like a church to me.
I entered it on soft foot,
Breath held like a cap in the hand.
It was quiet.
What God was there made himself felt,
Not listened to, in clean colours
That brought a moistening of the eye,
In movement of the wind over grass.

There were no prayers said. But stillness
Of the heart's passions—that was praise
Enough; and the mind's cession
Of its kingdom. I walked on,
Simple and poor, while the air crumbled
And broke on me generously as bread.

THERE

They are those that life happens to.
They didn't ask to be born
In those bleak farmsteads, but neither
Did they ask not. Life took the seed
And broadcast it upon the poor,
Rush-stricken soil, an experiment
In patience.
                    What is a man's
Price? For promises of a break
In the clouds; for harvests that are not all
Wasted; for one animal born
Healthy, where seven have died,
He will kneel down and give thanks
In a chapel whose stones are wrenched
From the moorland.
                    I have watched them bent

For hours over their trade,
Speechless, and have held my tongue
From its question. It was not my part
To show them, like a meddler from the town,
Their picture, nor the audiences
That look at them in pity or pride.

THE BELFRY

I have seen it standing up grey,
Gaunt, as though no sunlight
Could ever thaw out the music
Of its great bell; terrible
In its own way, for religion
Is like that. There are times
When a black frost is upon
One's whole being, and the heart
In its bone belfry hangs and is dumb.

But who is to know? Always,
Even in winter in the cold
Of a stone church, on his knees
Someone is praying, whose prayers fall
Steadily through the hard spell
Of weather that is between God
And himself. Perhaps they are warm rain
That brings the sun and afterwards flowers
On the raw graves and throbbing of bells.

ASIDE

Take heart, Prytherch.
Over you the planets stand,

And have seen more ills than yours.
This canker was in the bone
Before man bent to his image
In the pool's glass. Violence has been
And will be again. Between better
And worse is no bad place

For a labourer, whose lot is to seem
Stationary in traffic so fast.
Turn aside, I said; do not turn back.
There is no forward and no back
In the fields, only the year's two
Solstices, and patience between.

THE VISIT

She was small;
Composed in her way
Like music. She sat
In the chair I had not
Offered, smiling at my left
Shoulder. I waited on
For the sentences her smile
Sugared.
    That the tongue
Is a whip needed no
Proving. And yet her eye
Fondled me. It was clear
What anger brought her
To my door would not unleash
The coils. Instead she began
Rehearsing for her
Departure. As though ashamed
Of a long stay, she rose,
Touched the tips of my cold
Hand with hers and turned
To the closed door. I remember
Not opening it.

THE FACE

When I close my eyes, I can see it,
That bare hill with the man ploughing,
Corrugating that brown roof
Under a hard sky. Under him is the farm,
Anchored in its grass harbour;
And below that the valley
Sheltering its few folk,
With the school and the inn and the church,
The beginning, middle and end
Of their slow journey above ground.

He is never absent, but like a slave
Answers to the mind's bidding,
Endlessly ploughing, as though autumn
Were the one season he knew.
Sometimes he pauses to look down
To the grey farmhouse, but no signals
Cheer him; there is no applause
for his long wrestling with the angel
Of no name. I can see his eye
That expects nothing, that has the rain's
Colourlessness. His hands are broken
But not his spirit. He is like bark
Weathering on the tree of his kind.

He will go on; that much is certain.
Beneath him tenancies of the fields
Will change; machinery turn
All to noise. But on the walls
Of the mind's gallery that face
With the hills framing it will hang
Unglorified, but stern like the soil.

IN CHURCH

Often I try
To analyse the quality
Of its silences. Is this where God hides
From my searching? I have stopped to listen,
After the few people have gone,
To the air recomposing itself
For vigil. It has waited like this
Since the stones grouped themselves about it.
These are the hard ribs
Of a body that our prayers have failed
To animate. Shadows advance
From their corners to take possession
Of places the light held
For an hour. The bats resume
Their business. The uneasiness of the pews
Ceases. There is no other sound
In the darkness but the sound of a man
Breathing, testing his faith
On emptiness, nailing his questions
One by one to an untenanted cross.

CAREERS

Fifty-two years,
most of them taken in
growing or in the
illusion of it—what does the mem-
ory number as one's
property? The broken elbow?
The lost toy? The pain has
vanished, but the soft flesh
that suffered it is mine still.

There is a house with
a face mooning at the glass

of windows. Those eyes—I look
at not with them, but something of
their melancholy I
begin to lay claim to as my own.

A boy in school:
his lessons are
my lessons, his
punishments I learn to deserve.
I stand up in him,
tall as I am
now, but without per-
spective. Distant objects
are too distant, yet will arrive
soon. How his words
muddle me; how my deeds
betray him. That is not
our intention; but where I should
be one with him, I am one now
with another. Before I had time
to complete myself, I let her share
in the building. This that I am
now—too many
labourers. What is mine is
not mine only: her love, her
child wait for my slow
signature. Son, from the mirror
you hold to me I turn
to recriminate. That likeness
you are at work upon—it hurts.

NO

And one said, This man can sing;
Let's listen to him. But the other,
Dirt on his mind, said, No, let's
Queer him. And the first, being weak,

Consented. So the Thing came
Nearer him, and its breath caused
Him to retch, and none knew why.
But he rested for one long month,
And after began to sing
For gladness, and the Thing stood,
Letting him, for a year, for two;
Then put out its raw hand
And touched him, and the wound took
Over, and the nurses wiped off
The poetry from his cracked lips.

ST JULIAN AND THE LEPER

Though all ran from him, he did not
Run, but awaited
Him with his arms
Out, his ears stopped
To his bell, his alarmed
Crying. He lay down
With him there, sharing his sores'
Stench, the quarantine
Of his soul; contaminating
Himself with a kiss,
With the love that
Our science has disinfected.

CONCESSION

Not that he brought flowers
Except for the eyes' blue,
Perishable ones, or that his hands,
Famed for kindness were put then
To such usage; but rather that, going

Through flowers later, she yet could feel
These he spared perhaps for my sake.

SHRINE AT CAPE CLEAR

She is more white than the sea's
Purest spray, and colder
To touch. She is nourished
By salt winds, and the prayers
Of the drowned break on her. She smiles
At the stone angels, who have turned
From the sea's truth to worship
The mystery of her dumb child.

The bay brings her the tribute
Of its silences. The ocean has left
An offering of the small flowers
Of its springs; but the men read,
Beyond the harbour on the horizon,
The fury of its obituaries.

THE FISHERMAN

A simple man,
He liked the crease on the water
His cast made, but had no pity
For the broken backbone
Of water or fish.

One of his pleasures, thirsty,
Was to ask a drink
At the hot farms;
Leaving with a casual thank you,
As though they owed it him.

I could have told of the living water
That springs pure.
He would have smiled then,
Dancing his speckled fly in the shallows,
Not understanding.

AFTER THE LECTURE

I am asking the difficult question. I need help.
I'm not asking from ill will.
I have no desire to see you coping
Or not coping with the unmanageable coils
Of a problem frivolously called up.
I've read your books, had glimpses of a climate
That is rigorous, though not too hard
For the spirit. I may have grown
Since reading them; there is no scale
To judge by, neither is the soul
Measurable. I know all the tropes
Of religion, how God is not there
To go to; how time is what we buy
With his absence, and how we look
Through the near end of the binocular at pain,
Evil, deformity. I have tried
Bandaging my sharp eyes
With humility, but still the hearing
Of the ear holds; from as far off as Tibet
The cries come.
                From one not to be penned
In a concept, and differing in kind
From the human; whose attributes are the negations
Of thought; who holds us at bay with
His symbols, the opposed emblems
Of hawk and dove, what can my prayers win
For the kindred, souls brought to the bone
To be tortured, and burning, burning
Through history with their own strange light?

SAILORS' HOSPITAL

It was warm
Inside, but there was
Pain there. I came out
Into the cold wind
Of April. There were birds
In the brambles' old,
Jagged iron, with one striking
Its small song. To the west,
Rising from the grey
Water, leaning one
On another were the town's
Houses. Who first began
That refuse: time's waste
Growing at the edge
Of the clean sea? Some sailor,
Fetching up on the
Shingle before wind
Or current, made it his
Harbour, hung up his clothes
In the sunlight; found women
To breed from—those sick men
His descendants. Every day
Regularly the tide
Visits them with its salt
Comfort; their wounds are shrill
In the rigging of the
Tall ships.
              With clenched thoughts,
That not even the sky's
Daffodil could persuade
To open, I turned back
To the nurses in their tugging
At him, as he drifted
Away on the current
Of his breath, further and further,
Out of hail of our love.

RESERVOIRS

There are places in Wales I don't go:
Reservoirs that are the subconscious
Of a people, troubled far down
With gravestones, chapels, villages even;
The serenity of their expression
Revolts me; it is a pose
For strangers, a watercolour's appeal
To the mass, instead of the poem's
Harsher conditions. There are the hills,
Too; gardens gone under the scum
Of the forests; and the smashed faces
Of the farms with the stone trickle
Of their tears down the hills' side.

Where can I go, then, from the smell
Of decay, from the putrefying of a dead
Nation? I have walked the shore
For an hour and seen the English
Scavenging among the remains
Of our culture, covering the sand
Like the tide and, with the roughness
Of the tide, elbowing our language
Into the grave that we have dug for it.

THE PRIEST

The priest picks his way
Through the parish. Eyes watch him
From windows, from the farms;
Hearts wanting him to come near.
The flesh rejects him.

Women, pouring from the black kettle,
Stir up the whirling tea-grounds
Of their thoughts; offer him a dark
Filling in their smiling sandwich.

Priests have a long way to go.
The people wait for them to come
To them over the broken glass
Of their vows, making them pay
With their sweat's coinage for their correction.

He goes up a green lane
Through growing birches; lambs cushion
His vision. He comes slowly down
In the dark, feeling the cross warp
In his hands; hanging on it his thought's icicles.

'Crippled soul', do you say? looking at him
From the mind's height; 'limping through life
On his prayers. There are other people
In the world, sitting at table
Contented, though the broken body
And the shed blood are not on the menu'.

'Let it be so', I say. 'Amen and amen'.

KNEELING

Moments of great calm,
Kneeling before an altar
Of wood in a stone church
In summer, waiting for the God
To speak; the air a staircase
For silence; the sun's light
Ringing me, as though I acted
A great role. And the audiences
Still; all that close throng
Of spirits waiting, as I,
For the message.
                    Prompt me, God;
But not yet. When I speak,
Though it be you who speak
Through me, something is lost.
The meaning is in the waiting.

TENANCIES

This is pain's landscape.
A savage agriculture is practised
Here; every farm has its
Grandfather or grandmother, gnarled hands
On the cheque-book, a long, slow
Pull on the placenta about the neck.
Old lips monopolise the talk
When a friend calls. The children listen
From the kitchen; the children march
With angry patience against the dawn.
They are waiting for someone to die
Whose name is as bitter as the soil
They handle. In clear pools
In the furrows they watch themselves grow old
To the terrible accompaniment of the song
Of the blackbird, that promises them love.

NO, SEÑOR

We were out in the hard country.
The railroads kept crossing our path,
Signed with important names,
Salamanca to Madrid,
Malaga to Barcelona.
Sometimes an express went by,
Tubular in the newest fashion;
The faces were a blurred frieze,
A hundred or so city people
Digesting their latest meal,
Over coffee, over a cigarette,
Discussing the news from Viet Nam,
Fondling imaginary wounds
Of the last war, honouring themselves
In the country to which they belonged
By proxy. Their landscape slipped by

On a spool. We saw the asses
Hobbling upon the road
To the village, no Don Quixote
Upon their backs, but all the burden
Of a poor land, the weeds and grasses
Of the mesa. The men walked
Beside them; there was no sound
But the hoarse music of the bells.

COTO DOÑANA

I don't know; ask the place.
It was there when we found it:
Sand mostly, and bushes, too;
Some of them with dry flowers.
The map indicates a lake;
We thought we saw it from the top
Of a sand-dune, but walking brought it
No nearer.
           There are great birds
There that stain the sand
With their shadows, and snakes coil
Their necklaces about the bones
Of the carrion. At night the wild
Boars plough by their tusks'
Moonlight, and fierce insects
Sing, drilling for the blood
Of the humans, whom time's sea
Has left there to ride and dream.

LOOK

Look, here are two cronies, let's
Listen to them as the wind
Creeps under their clothes and the rain

Mixes with the bright moisture
Of their noses. They are saying,
Each in his own way, 'I am dying
And want to live. I am alive
And wish to die'. And for the same
Reason, that they have no belief
In a God who made the world
For misery and for the streams of pain
To flow in. Mildew and pus and decay
They deal in, and feed on mucous
And wind, diet of a wet land. So
They fester and, met now by this tree,
Complain, voices of the earth, talking,
Not as we wanted it to talk,
Who have been reared on its reflections
In art or had its behaviour
Seen to. We must dip belief
Not in dew nor in the cool fountain
Of beech buds, but in seas
Of manure through which they squelch
To the bleakness of their assignations.

ART HISTORY

They made the grey stone
Blossom, setting it on a branch
Of the mind; airy cathedrals
Grew, trembling at the tip
Of their breathing; delicate palaces
Hung motionless in the gold,
Unbelievable sunrise. They praised
With rapt forms such as the blind hand
Dreamed, journeying to its sad
Nuptials. We come too late
On the scene, pelted with the stone
Flowers' bitter confetti.

THE SMALL WINDOW

In Wales there are jewels
To gather, but with the eye
Only. A hill lights up
Suddenly; a field trembles
With colour and goes out
In its turn; in one day
You can witness the extent
Of the spectrum and grow rich

With looking. Have a care;
This wealth is for the few
And chosen. Those who crowd
A small window dirty it
With their breathing, though sublime
And inexhaustible the view.

AGAIN

What to do? It's the old boredom
Come again: indolent grass,
Wind creasing the water
Hardly at all; a bird floating
Round and round. For one hour
I have known Eden, the still place
We hunger for. My hand lay
Innocent; the mind was idle.

Nothing has changed; the day goes on
With its business, watching itself
In a calm mirror. Yet I know now
I am ready for the sly tone
Of the serpent, ready to climb
My branches after the same fruit.

BURGOS

Nightingales crackled in the frost
At Burgos. The day dawned fiercely
On the parched land, on the fields to the east
Of the city, bitter with sage
And thistle. Lonely bells called
From the villages; no one answered
Them but the sad priests, fingering
Their beads, praying for the lost people
Of the soil. Everywhere were the slow
Donkeys, carrying silent men
To the mesa to reap their bundles
Of dried grass. In the air an eagle
Circled, shadowless as the God
Who made that country and drinks its blood.

STUDY

The flies walk upon the roof top.
The student's eyes are too keen
To miss them. The young girls walk
In the roadway; the wind ruffles
Their skirts. The student does not look.
He sees only the flies spread their wings
And take off into the sunlight
Without sound. There is nothing to do
Now but read in his book
Of how young girls walked in the roadway
In Tyre, and how young men
Sailed off into the red west
For gold, writing dry words
To the music the girls sang.

THAT

It will always win.
Other men will come as I have
To stand here and beat upon it
As on a door, and ask for love,
For compassion, for hatred even; for anything
Rather than this blank indifference,
Than the neutrality of its answers, if they can be called
    answers,
These grey skies, these wet fields,
With the wind's winding-sheet upon them.

And endlessly the days go on
With their business. Lovers make their appearance
And vanish. The germ finds its way
From the grass to the snail to the liver to the grass.
The shadow of the tree falls
On our acres like a crucifixion,
With a bird singing in the branches
What its shrill species has always sung,
Hammering its notes home
One by one into our brief flesh.

THE PLACE

Summer is here.
Once more the house has its
Spray of martins, Proust's fountain
Of small birds, whose light shadows
Come and go in the sunshine
Of the lawn as thoughts do
In the mind. Watching them fly
Is my business, not as a man vowed
To science, who counts their returns
To the rafters, or sifts their droppings

For facts, recording the wave-length
Of their screaming; my method is so
To have them about myself
Through the hours of this brief
Season and to fill with their
Movement, that it is I they build
In and bring up their young
To return to after the bitter
Migrations, knowing the site
Inviolate through its outward changes.

ONCE

God looked at space and I appeared,
Rubbing my eyes at what I saw.
The earth smoked, no birds sang:
There were no footprints on the beaches
Of the hot sea, no creatures in it.
God spoke. I hid myself in the side
Of the mountain.
                              As though born again
I stepped out into the cool dew,
Trying to remember the fire sermon,
Astonished at the mingled chorus
Of weeds and flowers. In the brown bark
Of the Trees I saw the many faces
Of life, forms hungry for birth,
Mouthing at me. I held my way
To the light, inspecting my shadow
Boldly; and in the late morning
You, rising towards me out of the depths
Of myself. I took your hand,
Remembering you, and together,
Confederates of the natural day,
We went forth to meet the Machine.

PETITION

And I standing in the shade
Have seen it a thousand times
Happen: first theft, then murder;
Rape; the rueful acts
Of the blind hand. I have said
New prayers, or said the old
In a new way. Seeking the poem
In the pain, I have learned
Silence is best, paying for it
With my conscience. I am eyes
Merely, witnessing virtue's
Defeat; seeing the young born
Fair, knowing the cancer
Awaits them. One thing I have asked
Of the disposer of the issues
Of life: that truth should defer
To beauty. It was not granted.

THIS ONE

Oh, I know it: the long story,
The ecstasies, the mutilations;
Crazed, pitiable creatures
Imagining themselves a Napoleon,
A Jesus; letting their hair grow,
Shaving it off; gorging themselves
On a dream; kindling
A new truth, withering by it.

While patiently this poor farmer
Purged himself in his strong sweat,
Ploughing under the tall boughs
Of the tree of the knowledge of
Good and evil, watching its fruit
Ripen, abstaining from it.

ECHOES

What is this? said God. The obstinacy
Of its refusal to answer
Enraged him. He struck it
Those great blows it resounds
With still. It glowered at
Him, but remained dumb,
Turning on its slow axis
Of pain, reflecting the year
In its seasons. Nature bandaged
Its wounds. Healing in
The smooth sun, it became
Fair. God looked at it
Again, reminded of
An intention. They shall answer
For you, he said. And at once
There were trees with birds
Singing, and through the trees
Animals wandered, drinking
Their own scent, conceding
An absence. Where are you?
He called, and riding the echo
The shapes came, slender
As trees, but with white hands,
Curious to build. On the altars
They made him the red blood
Told what he wished to hear.

INVITATION

And one voice says: Come
Back to the rain and manure
Of Siloh, to the small talk,
Of the wind, and the chapel's

Temptation; to the pale,
Sickly half-smile of
The daughter of the village
Grocer. The other says: Come

To the streets, where the pound
Sings and the doors open
To its music, with life
Like an express train running

To time. And I stay
Here, listening to them, blowing
On the small soul in my
Keeping with such breath as I have.

PERIOD

It was a time when wise men
Were not silent, but stifled
By vast noise. They took refuge
In books that were not read.

Two counsellors had the ear
Of the public. One cried 'Buy'
Day and night, and the other,
More plausibly, 'Sell your repose'.

NO ANSWER

But the chemicals in
My mind were not
Ready, so I let
Him go on, dissolving
The word on my
Tongue. Friend, I had said,

Life is too short for
Religion; it takes time
To prepare a sacrifice
For the God. Give yourself
To science that reveals
All, asking no pay
For it. Knowledge is power;
The old oracle
Has not changed. The nucleus
In the atom awaits
Our bidding. Come forth,
We cry, and the dust spreads
Its carpet. Over the creeds
And masterpieces our wheels go.

SONG

I choose white, but with
Red on it, like the snow
In winter with its few
Holly berries and the one

Robin, that is a fire
To warm by and like Christ
Comes to us in his weakness,
But with a sharp song.

DIGEST

Mostly it was wars
With their justification
Of the surrender of values
For which they fought. Between
Them they laid their plans

For the next, exempted
From compact by the machine's
Exigencies. Silence
Was out of date; wisdom consisted
In a revision of the strict code
Of the spirit. To keep moving
Was best; to bring the arrival
Nearer departure; to synchronise
The applause, as the public images
Stepped on and off the stationary
Aircraft. The labour of the years
Was over; the children were heirs
To an instant existence. They fed the machine
Their questions, knowing the answers
Already, unable to apply them.

ACTING

Being unwise enough to have married her
I never knew when she was not acting.
'I love you' she would say; I heard the audiences
Sigh. 'I hate you'; I could never be sure
They were still there. She was lovely. I
Was only the looking-glass she made up in.
I husbanded the rippling meadow
Of her body. Their eyes grazed nightly upon it.

Alone now on the brittle platform
Of herself she is playing her last rôle.
It is perfect. Never in all her career
Was she so good. And yet the curtain
Has fallen. My charmer, come out from behind
It to take the applause. Look, I am clapping too.

PAVANE

Convergences
Of the spirit! What
Century, love? I,
Too; you remember—
Brescia? This sunlight reminds
Of the brocade. I dined
Long. And now the music
Of darkness in your eyes
Sounds. But Brescia,
And the spreading foliage
Of smoke! With Yeats' birds
Grown hoarse.
                    Artificer
Of the years, is this
Your answer? The long dream
Unwound; we followed
Through time to the tryst
With ourselves. But wheels roll
Between and the shadow
Of the plane falls. The
Victim remains
Nameless on the tall
Steps. Master, I
Do not wish, I do not wish
To continue.

CAIN

Abel looked at the wound
His brother had dealt him, and loved him
For it. Cain saw that look
And struck him again. The blood cried
On the ground; God listened to it.
He questioned Cain. But Cain answered:

Who made the blood? I offered you
Clean things: the blond hair
Of the corn; the knuckled vegetables; the
Flowers; things that did not publish
Their hurt, that bled
Silently. You would not accept them.

And God said: It was part of myself
He gave me. The lamb was torn
From my own side. The limp head,
The slow fall of red tears—they
Were like a mirror to me in which I beheld
My reflection. I anointed myself
In readiness for the journey
To the doomed tree you were at work upon.

VIA NEGATIVA

Why no! I never thought other than
That God is that great absence
In our lives, the empty silence
Within, the place where we go
Seeking, not in hope to
Arrive or find. He keeps the interstices
In our knowledge, the darkness
Between stars. His are the echoes
We follow, the footprints he has just
Left. We put our hands in
His side hoping to find
It warm. We look at people
And places as though he had looked
At them, too; but miss the reflection.

THE HEARTH

In front of the fire
With you, the folk song
Of the wind in the chimney and the sparks'
Embroidery of the soot—eternity
Is here in this small room,
In intervals that our love
Widens; and outside
Us is time and the victims
Of time, travellers
To a new Bethlehem, statesmen
And scientists with their hands full
Of the gifts that destroy.

RUINS

And this was a civilisation
That came to nothing—he spurned with his toe
The slave-coloured dust. We breathed it in
Thankfully, oxygen to our culture.

Somebody found a curved bone
In the ruins. A king's probably,
He said. Impertinent courtiers
We eyed it, the dropped kerchief of time.

THE ISLAND

And God said, I will build a church here
And cause this people to worship me,
And afflict them with poverty and sickness
In return for centuries of hard work
And patience. And its walls shall be hard as

Their hearts, and its windows let in the light
Grudgingly, as their minds do, and the priest's words be
    drowned
By the wind's caterwauling. All this I will do,

Said God, and watch the bitterness in their eyes
Grow, and their lips suppurate with
Their prayers. And their women shall bring forth
On my altars, and I will choose the best
Of them to be thrown back into the sea.

And that was only on one island.

POSTSCRIPT

As life improved, their poems
Grew sadder and sadder. Was there oil
For the machine? It was
The vinegar in the poets' cup.

The tins marched to the music
Of the conveyor belt. A billion
Mouths opened. Production,
Production, the wheels

Whistled. Among the forests
Of metal the one human
Sound was the lament of
The poets for deciduous language.

THE RIVER

And the cobbled water
Of the stream with the trout's indelible
Shadows that winter
Has not erased—I walk it

Again under a clean
Sky with the fish, speckled like thrushes,
Silently singing among the weed's
Branches.
          I bring the heart
Not the mind to the interpretation
Of their music, letting the stream
Comb me, feeling it fresh
In my veins, revisiting the sources
That are as near now
As on the morning I set out from them.

REMEDIES

There were people around;
I would have spoken with them.
But the situation had got beyond
Language. Machines were invented
To cope, but they also were limited
By our expectations. Men stared
With a sort of growing resentment
At life that was ubiquitous and
Unseizable. A sense of betrayal
At finding themselves alive at all
Maddened the young; the older,
Following the narrowing perspectives
Of art, squinted at where a god died.
Between fierce alternatives
There was need as always of a third
Way. History was the proliferation
Of the offerers of such. Fortunes were made
On the ability to disappoint.

FEMALE

It was the other way round:
God waved his slow wand
And the creature became a woman,
Imperceptibly, retaining its body,
Nose, brow, lips, eyes,
And the face that was like a flower
On the neck's stem. The man turned to her,
Crazy with the crushed smell
Of her hair; and her eyes warned him
To keep off. And she spoke to him with the voice
Of his own conscience, and rippled there
In the shade. So he put his hands
To his face, while her forked laughter
Played on him, and his leaves fell
Silently round him, and he hung there
On himself, waiting for the God to see.

ALL RIGHT

I look. You look
Away. No colour,
No ruffling of the brow's
Surface betrays
Your feeling. As though I
Were not here; as
Though you were your own
Mirror, you arrange yourself
For the play. My eyes'
Adjectives; the way that
I scan you; the
Conjunction the flesh
Needs—all these
Are as nothing
To you. Serene, cool,

Motionless, no statue
Could show less
The impression of
My regard. Madam, I
Grant the artistry
Of your part. Let us
Consider it, then,
A finished performance.

SOLILOQUY

And God thought: Pray away,
Creatures; I'm going to destroy
It. The mistake's mine,
If you like. I have blundered
Before; the glaciers erased
My error.
             I saw them go
Further than you—palaces,
Missiles. My privacy
Was invaded; then the flaw
Took over; they allied themselves
With the dust. Winds blew away
Their pasture. Their bones signalled
From the desert to me
In vain.
            After the dust, fire;
The earth burned. I have forgotten
How long, but the fierce writing
Seduced me. I blew with my cool
Breath; the vapour condensed
In the hollows. The sun was torn
From my side. Out of the waters
You came, as subtle
As water, with your mineral
Poetry and promises

Of obedience. I listened to you
Too long. Within the churches
You built me you genuflected
To the machine. Where will it
Take you from the invisible
Viruses, the personnel
Of the darkness that do my will?

THAT DAY

Stopped the car, asked a man the way
To some place; he rested on it
Smiling, an impression of charm
As of ripe fields; talking to us
He held a reflection of sky
In his brushed eyes. We lost interest
In the way, seeing him old
And content, feeling the sun's warmth
In his voice, watching the swallows
Above him—thirty years back
To this summer. Knowing him gone,
We wander the same flower-bordered road,
Seeing the harvest ripped from the land,
Deafened by the planes' orchestra;
Unable to direct the lost travellers
Or convince them this a good place to be.

H'M

and one said
speak to us of love
and the preacher opened
his mouth and the word God
fell out so they tried

again speak to us
of God then but the preacher
was silent reaching
his arms out but the little
children the ones with
big bellies and bow
legs that were like
a razor shell
were too weak to come

THE KINGDOM

It's a long way off but inside it
There are quite different things going on:
Festivals at which the poor man
Is king and the consumptive is
Healed; mirrors in which the blind look
At themselves and love looks at them
Back; and industry is for mending
The bent bones and the minds fractured
By life. It's a long way off, but to get
There takes no time and admission
Is free, if you will purge yourself
Of desire, and present yourself with
Your need only and the simple offering
Of your faith, green as a leaf.

THE COMING

And God held in his hand
A small globe. Look, he said.
The son looked. Far off,
As through water, he saw
A scorched land of fierce

Colour. The light burned
There; crusted buildings
Cast their shadows: a bright
Serpent, a river
Uncoiled itself, radiant
With slime.
                    On a bare
Hill a bare tree saddened
The sky. Many people
Held out their thin arms
To it, as though waiting
For a vanished April
To return to its crossed
Boughs. The son watched
Them. Let me go there, he said.

OTHER

It was perfect. He could do
Nothing about it. Its waters
Were as clear as his own eye. The grass
Was his breath. The mystery
Of the dark earth was what went on
In himself. He loved and
Hated it with a parent's
Conceit, admiring his own
Work, resenting its
Independence. There were trysts
In the greenwood at which
He was not welcome. Youths and girls,
Fondling the pages of
A strange book, awakened
His envy. The mind achieved
What the heart could not. He began planning
The destruction of the long peace
Of the place. The machine appeared

In the distance, singing to itself
Of money. Its song was the web
They were caught in, men and women
Together. The villages were as flies
To be sucked empty.

                    God secreted
A tear. Enough, enough,
He commanded, but the machine
Looked at him and went on singing.

THE FAIR

The idiot goes round and around
With his brother in a bumping car
At the fair. The famous idiot
Smile hangs over the car's edge,
Illuminating nothing. This is mankind
Being taken for a ride by a rich
Relation. The responses are fixed:
Bump, smile; bump, smile. And the current

Is generated by the smooth flow
Of the shillings. This is an orchestra
Of steel with the constant percussion
Of laughter. But where he should be laughing
Too, his features are split open, and look!
Out of the cracks come warm, human tears.

MADAM

And if you ask her
she has no name;
but her eyes say:
Water is cold.

She is three years old
and willing to kiss;
but her lips say:
Apples are sour.

THE EARTH DOES ITS BEST FOR HIM

The paintings are under glass,
or in dry rooms it is difficult
to breathe in; they are tired
of returning the hard stare
of eyes. The sculptures are smooth
from familiarity. There is a smell
of dust, the precipitation
of culture from dead skies.

I return to Lleyn,
repository of the condescension
of time. Through the car's
open windows the scent of hay
comes. It is incense, the seasonally
renewed offering of the live earth.

THE HAND

It was a hand. God looked at it
and looked away. There was a coldness
about his heart, as though the hand
clasped it. As at the end
of a dark tunnel, he saw cities
the hand would build, engines
that it would raze them with. His sight
dimmed. Tempted to undo the joints
of the fingers, he picked it up.

But the hand wrestled with him. 'Tell
me your name,' it cried, 'and I will write it
in bright gold. Are there not deeds
to be done, children to make, poems
to be written? The world
is without meaning, awaiting
my coming.' But God, feeling the nails
in his side, the unnerving warmth
of the contact, fought on in
silence. This was the long war with himself
always foreseen, the question not
to be answered. What is the hand
for? The immaculate conception
preceding the delivery
of the first tool? 'I let you go,'
he said, 'but without blessing.
Messenger to the mixed things
of your making, tell them I am.'

THE WORD

A pen appeared, and the god said:
'Write what it is to be
man.' And my hand hovered
long over the bare page,

until there, like footprints
of the lost traveller, letters
took shape on the page's
blankness, and I spelled out

the word 'lonely'. And my hand moved
to erase it; but the voices
of all those waiting at life's
window cried out loud: 'It is true.'

OUT THERE

It is another country.
There is no speech there such
as we know; even the colours
                    are different.
When the residents use their eyes,
it is not shapes they see but the distance
between them. If they go,
it is not in a traveller's
usual direction, but sideways and
out through the mirror of a refracted
timescale. If you met them early,
you would recognize them by an absence
of shadow. Your problems
                    are in their past;
those they are about to solve
are what you are incapable
of conceiving. In experiments
in outbreeding, under the growing microscope
of the mind, they are isolating
the human virus and burning it
up in the fierceness of their detachment.

AMEN

It was all arranged:
the virgin with child, the birth
in Bethlehem, the arid journey uphill
to Jerusalem. The prophets foretold
it, the scriptures conditioned him
to accept it. Judas went to his work
with his sour kiss; what else
could he do?
                    A wise old age,
the honours awarded for lasting,

are not for a saviour. He had
to be killed; salvation acquired
by an increased guilt. The tree,
with its roots in the mind's dark,
was divinely planted, the original fork
in existence. There is no meaning in life,
unless men can be found to reject
love. God needs his martyrdom.
The mild eyes stare from the Cross
in perverse triumph. What does he care
that the people's offerings are so small?

THAT PLACE

I served on a dozen committees;
talked hard, said little, shared the applause
at the end. Picking over
the remains later, we agreed power
was not ours, launched our invective
at others, the anonymous wielders
of such. Life became small, grey,
the smell of interiors. Occasions
on which a clean air entered our nostrils
off swept seas were instances
we sought to recapture. One particular
time after a harsh morning
of rain, the clouds lifted, the wind
fell; there was a resurrection
of nature, and we there to emerge
with it into the anointed
air. I wanted to say to you: 'We
will remember this.' But tenses
were out of place on that green
island, ringed with the rain's
bow, that we had found and would spend
the rest of our lives looking for.

RELAY

I switch on, tune in—
the marvellous languages
of the peoples of the planet,
discussing the weather! Thousands of years
speech was evolving—that line of trees
on the hill slope has the illusion
of movement. I think of man
on his mountain; he has paused
now for lack of the oxygen
of the spirit; the easier options
surround him, the complacencies of being
half-way up. He needs some breath
from the summit, a stench rising
to him from the valley from
which he has toiled to release
his potential; a memory rather
of those bright flags, that other
climbers of other mountains
have planted and gone
their way, not down but on
up the incline of their choosing.

GOOD FRIDAY

It was quiet. What had the sentry
to cry, but that it was the ninth hour
and all was not well? The darkness
began to lift, but it was not the mind

was illumined. The carpenter
had done his work well to sustain
the carpenter's burden; the Cross an example
of the power of art to transcend timber.

POSTE RESTANTE

I want you to know how it was,
whether the Cross grinds into dust
under men's wheels or shines brightly
as a monument to a new era.

There was a church and one man
served it, and few worshipped
there in the raw light on the hill
in winter, moving among the stones
fallen about them like the ruins
of a culture they were too weak
to replace, too poor themselves
to do anything but wait
for the ending of a life
they had not asked for.
                        The priest would come
and pull on the hoarse bell nobody
heard, and enter that place
of darkness, sour with the mould
of the years. And the spider would run
from the chalice, and the wine lie
there for a time, cold and unwanted
by all but he, while the candles
guttered as the wind picked
at the roof. And he would see
over that bare meal his face
staring at him from the cracked glass
of the window, with the lips moving
like those of an inhabitant of
a world beyond this.
                        And so back
to the damp vestry to the book
where he would scratch his name and the date
he could hardly remember, Sunday
by Sunday, while the place sank
to its knees and the earth turned

from season to season like the wheel
of a great foundry to produce
you, friend, who will know what happened.

DEGAS: WOMAN COMBING

So the hair, too,
            can be played?

She lets it down
            and combs a sonata

from it: brown cello
            of hair, with the arm

bowing. Painter,
            who with your quick

brush, gave us this silent
            music, there is nothing

that you left out.
            The blues and greens,

the abandoned snowfall
            of her shift, the light

on her soft flesh tell us
            from what score she performs.

THE CHAPEL

A little aside from the main road,
becalmed in a last-century greyness,
there is the chapel, ugly, without the appeal
to the tourist to stop his car
and visit it. The traffic goes by,

and the river goes by, and quick shadows
of clouds, too, and the chapel settles
a little deeper into the grass.

But here once on an evening like this,
in the darkness that was about
his hearers, a preacher caught fire
and burned steadily before them
with a strange light, so that they saw
the splendour of the barren mountains
about them and sang their amens
fiercely, narrow but saved
in a way that men are not now.

THE CASUALTY

I had forgotten
   the old quest for truth
     I was here for. Other cares

held me: urgencies
   of the body; a girl
     beckoned; money

had never appeared
   so ethereal; it was God's blood
     circulating in the veins

of creation; I partook
   of it like Communion, lost
     myself on my way

home, with the varying voices
   on call. Moving backward
     into a receding

future, I lost the use
   of perspective, borrowing poetry
     to buy my children

their prose. The past was a poor
king, rendering his crown down
for the historian. Every day
I went on with that
metallic warfare in which
the one casualty is love.

PROBING

No one would know you had lived,
but for my discovery
of the anonymous undulation
of your grave, like the early swelling
of the belly of a woman
who is with child. And if I entered
it now, I would find your bones
huddled together, but without
flesh, their ruined architecture
a reproach, the skull luminous
but not with thought.
                    Would it help us to learn
what you were called in your forgotten
language? Are not our jaws
frail for the sustaining of the consonants'
weight? Yet they were balanced
on tongues like ours, echoed
in the ears' passages, in intervals when
the volcano was silent. How
tenderly did the woman handle
them, as she leaned her haired body
to yours? Where are the instruments
of your music, the pipe of hazel, the
bull's horn, the interpreters
of your loneliness on this
ferocious planet?

We are domesticating
it slowly; but at times it rises
against us, so that we see again
the primeval shadows you built
your fire amongst. We are cleverer
than you; our nightmares
are intellectual. But we never awaken
from the compulsiveness of the mind's
stare into the lenses' furious interiors.

THE FLOWER

I asked for riches.
You gave me the earth, the sea,
                        the immensity
of the broad sky. I looked at them
and learned I must withdraw
            to possess them. I gave my eyes
            and my ears, and dwelt
in a soundless darkness
                        in the shadow
        of your regard.
                        The soul
        grew in me, filling me
with its fragrance.
                    Men came
to me from the four
            winds to hear me speak
            of the unseen flower by which
I sat, whose roots were not
in the soil, nor its petals the colour
of the wide sea; that was
            its own species with its own
            sky over it, shot
with the rainbow of your coming and going.

FARMING PETER

and there the scarecrow walked
over the surface of the brown
breakers tattered like Christ
himself and the man went
at his call with the fathoms
under him and because
of his faith in the creation
of his own hands he was
buoyed up floundering
but never sinking scalded
by the urine of the skies deaf
to the voices calling from
the high road telling him
his Saviour's face was of straw.

ANN GRIFFITH

So God spoke to her,
she the poor girl from the village
without learning. 'Play me,'
he said, 'on the white keys
of your body. I have seen you dance
for the bridegrooms that were not
to be, while I waited for you
under the ripening boughs of
the myrtle. These people know me
only in the thin hymns of
the mind, in the arid sermons
and prayers. I am the live God,
nailed fast to the old tree
of a nation by its unreal
tears. I thirst, I thirst
for the spring water. Draw it up
for me from your heart's well and I will change
it to wine upon your unkissed lips.'

THE MOON IN LLEYN

The last quarter of the moon
of Jesus gives way
to the dark; the serpent
digests the egg. Here
on my knees in this stone
church, that is full only
of the silent congregation
of shadows and the sea's
sound, it is easy to believe
Yeats was right. Just as though
choirs had not sung, shells
have swallowed them; the tide laps
at the Bible; the bell fetches
no people to the brittle miracle
of the bread. The sand is waiting
for the running back of the grains
in the wall into its blond
glass. Religion is over, and
what will emerge from the body
of the new moon, no one
can say.
          But a voice sounds
in my ear: Why so fast,
mortal? These very seas
are baptized. The parish
has a saint's name time cannot
unfrock. In cities that
have outgrown their promise people
are becoming pilgrims
again, if not to this place,
then to the recreation of it
in their own spirits. You must remain
kneeling. Even as this moon
making its way through the earth's
cumbersome shadow, prayer, too,
has its phases.

ROUGH

God looked at the eagle that looked at
the wolf that watched the jack-rabbit
cropping the grass, green and curling
as God's beard. He stepped back;
it was perfect, a self-regulating machine
of blood and faeces. One thing was missing:
he skimmed off a faint reflection of himself
in sea-water; breathed air into it,
and set the red corpuscles whirling. It was not long
before the creature had the eagle, the wolf and
the jack-rabbit squealing for mercy. Only the grass
resisted. It used it to warm its imagination
by. God took a handful of small germs,
sowing them in the smooth flesh. It was curious,
the harvest: the limbs modelled an obscene
question, the head swelled, out of the eyes came
tears of pus. There was the sound
of thunder, the loud, uncontrollable laughter of
God, and in his side like an incurred stitch, Jesus.

VENEZIANO: THE ANNUNCIATION

The messenger is winged
                   and the girl
haloed a distance
              between them
and between them and us
down the long path the door
through which he has not
                 come
on his lips what all women
              desire to hear
in his hand the flowers that
           he has taken from her.

HILL CHRISTMAS

They came over the snow to the bread's
purer snow, fumbled it in their huge
hands, put their lips to it
like beasts, stared into the dark chalice
where the wine shone, felt it sharp
on their tongue, shivered as at a sin
remembered, and heard love cry
momentarily in their hearts' manger.

They rose and went back to their poor
holdings, naked in the bleak light
of December. Their horizon contracted
to the one small, stone-riddled field
with its tree, where the weather was nailing
the appalled body that had not asked to be born.

THE COMBAT

You have no name.
We have wrestled with you all
day, and now night approaches,
the darkness from which we emerged
seeking; and anonymous
you withdraw, leaving us nursing
our bruises, our dislocations.

For the failure of language
there is no redress. The physicists
tell us your size, the chemist
the ingredients of your
thinking. But who you are
does not appear, nor why
on the innocent marches
of vocabulary you should choose
to engage us, belabouring us

with your silence. We die, we die
with the knowledge that your resistance
is endless at the frontier of the great poem.

FFYNNON FAIR
(ST MARY'S WELL)

They did not divine it, but
they bequeathed it to us:
clear water, brackish at times,
complicated by the white frosts
of the sea, but thawing quickly.

Ignoring my image, I peer down
to the quiet roots of it, where
the coins lie, the tarnished offerings
of the people to the pure spirit
that lives there, that has lived there
always, giving itself up
to the thirsty, withholding
itself from the superstition
of others, who ask for more.

SOMEWHERE

Something to bring back to show
you have been there: a lock of God's
hair, stolen from him while he was
asleep; a photograph of the garden
of the spirit. As has been said,
the point of travelling is not
to arrive, but to return home
laden with pollen you shall work up
into the honey the mind feeds on.

What are our lives but harbours
we are continually setting out
from, airports at which we touch
down and remain in too briefly
to recognize what it is they remind
us of? And always in one
another we seek the proof
of experiences it would be worth dying for.

Surely there is a shirt of fire
this one wore, that is hung up now
like some rare fleece in the hall of heroes?
Surely these husbands and wives
have dipped their marriages in a fast
spring? Surely there exists somewhere,
as the justification for our looking for it,
the one light that can cast such shadows?

MARGED

Was she planned?
Or is this one of life's
throw-offs? Small, taken from school
young; put to minister
to a widowed mother, who keeps
her simple, she feeds the hens,
speaks their language, is one
of them, quick, easily
frightened, with sharp
eyes, ears. When I have
been there, she keeps her perch
on my mind. I would
stroke her feathers, quieten
her, say: 'Life is
like this.' But have I
the right, who have seen plainer

women with love
in abundance, with
freedom, with money to
hand? If there is one thing
she has, it is a bird's
nature, volatile
as a bird. But even
as those among whom she
lives and moves, who look at her
with their expectant
glances, song is denied her.

THUS

Whatever you imagine
has happened. No words
are unspoken, no actions
undone: wine poisoned

in the chalice, the corpses
raped. While Isaiah's
angel hither and thither
flies with his hot coal.

ALIVE

It is alive. It is you,
God. Looking out I can see
no death. The earth moves, the
sea moves, the wind goes
on its exuberant
journeys. Many creatures
reflect you, the flowers
your colour, the tides the precision

of your calculations. There
is nothing too ample
for you to overflow, nothing
so small that your workmanship
is not revealed. I listen
and it is you speaking.
I find the place where you lay
warm. At night, if I waken,
there are the sleepless conurbations
of the stars. The darkness
is the deepening shadow
of your presence; the silence a
process in the metabolism
of the being of love.

THE PRISONER

'Poems from prison! About
what?'
          'Life and God.' 'God
in prison? Friend, you trifle
with me. His face, perhaps,
at the bars, fading
like life.'
          'He came in
with the warder, striving
with him. Where else
did the severity of the man
spring from, but awareness
of a charity he must
overcome?'
          'The blows, then,
were God chastening
the beloved! Who
was the more blessed, the

dispenser or receiver
of them?'
             'It is the same
outside. Bars, walls
but make the perspective
clear. *Deus absconditus*!
We ransack the heavens,
the distance between
stars; the last place we look
is in prison, his hideout
in flesh and bone.'
                       'You believe,
then?'
             'The poems
are witness. If his world
contracted, it was to give birth
to the larger vision. Not meadows
empty of him, animal
eyes, impersonal
as glass, communicate
God. On the bare walls
of a cell the oppressor watches
the diminishing of his
human shadow, as
he withdraws from the light.'

MARRIAGE

I look up; you pass.
I have to reconcile your
existence and the meaning of it
with what I read: kings and queens
and their battles
for power. You have your battle,
too. I ask myself: Have

I been on your side? Lovelier
a dead queen than a live
wife? History worships
the fact but cannot remain
neutral. Because there are no kings
worthy of you; because poets
better than I are not here
to describe you; because time
is always too short, you must go by
now without mention, as unknown
to the future as to
the past, with one man's
eyes resting on you
in the interval of his concern.

MONTROSE

It is said that he went gaily to that scaffold,
dressed magnificently as a bridegroom,
his lace lying on him like white frost
in the windless morning of his courage.

His red blood was the water of life,
changed to wine at the wedding banquet;
the bride Scotland, the spirit dependent on
such for the consummation of her marriage.

THE BRIGHT FIELD

I have seen the sun break through
to illuminate a small field
for a while, and gone my way
and forgotten it. But that was the pearl
of great price, the one field that had

the treasure in it. I realize now
that I must give all that I have
to possess it. Life is not hurrying

on to a receding future, nor hankering after
an imagined past. It is the turning
aside like Moses to the miracle
of the lit bush, to a brightness
that seemed as transitory as your youth
once, but is the eternity that awaits you.

NOW

Men, who in their day
went down acknowledging
defeat, what would they say
now, where no superlatives
have meaning? What was failure
to them, our abandonment
of an ideal has turned
into high art. Could
they with foreknowledge have
been happy? Can we,
because there are levels
not yet descended to,
take comfort? Is it
sufficient for us
that we, like that minority
of our fellows in the hurrying
centuries, turning aside
re-enter the garden? What
is the serenity of art
worth without the angels
at the hot gates, whose sword
is time and our uneasy conscience?

LLANANNO

I often call there.
There are no poems in it
for me. But as a gesture
of independence of the speeding
traffic I am a part
of, I stop the car,
turn down the narrow path
to the river, and enter
the church with its clear reflection
beside it.
            There are few services
now; the screen has nothing
to hide. Face to face
with no intermediary
between me and God, and only the water's
quiet insistence on a time
older than man, I keep my eyes
open and am not dazzled,
so delicately does the light enter
my soul from the serene presence
that waits for me till I come next.

THE INTERROGATION

But the financiers will ask
in that day: Is it not better
to leave broken bank balances
behind us than broken heads?

And Christ recognizing the
new warriors will feel breaching
his healed side their terrible
pencil and the haemorrhage of its figures.

SEA-WATCHING

Grey waters, vast
        as an area of prayer
that one enters. Daily
        over a period of years
I have let the eye rest on them.
Was I waiting for something?
                    Nothing
but that continuous waving
        that is without meaning
occurred.
        Ah, but a rare bird is
rare. It is when one is not looking,
at times one is not there
                that it comes.
You must wear your eyes out,
as others their knees.
        I became the hermit
of the rocks, habited with the wind
and the mist. There were days,
so beautiful the emptiness
it might have filled,
              its absence
was as its presence; not to be told
any more, so single my mind
after its long fast,
          my watching from praying.

GOOD

The old man comes out on the hill
and looks down to recall earlier days
in the valley. He sees the stream shine,
the church stand, hears the litter of
children's voices. A chill in the flesh

tells him that death is not far off
now: it is the shadow under the great boughs
of life. His garden has herbs growing.
The kestrel goes by with fresh prey
in its claws. The wind scatters the scent
of wild beans. The tractor operates
on the earth's body. His grandson is there
ploughing; his young wife fetches him
cakes and tea and a dark smile. It is well.

THE LISTENER IN THE CORNER

Last night the talk
was of the relationship of the self
to God, to-night of God
to the self. The centuries
yawn. Alone in the corner
one sits whose silence persuades
of the pointlessness
of the discourse. He drinks
at another fountain that builds
itself equally from the dust of ruffians
and saints. Outside the wind
howls; the stars, that once
were the illuminated city
of the imagination, to him are fires
extinguished before the eyes' lenses
formed. The universe
is a large place with more of
darkness than light. But slowly
a web is spun there as minds like
his swing themselves to and fro.

BARN OWL

I

Mostly it is a pale
face hovering in the afterdraught
of the spirit, making both ends meet
on a scream. It is the breath
of the churchyard, the forming
of white frost in a believer,
when he would pray; it is soft
feathers camouflaging a machine.

It repeats itself year
after year in its offspring,
the staring pupils it teaches
its music to, that is the voice
of God in the darkness cursing himself
fiercely for his lack of love.

2

and there the owl happens
like white frost as
cruel and as silent
and the time on its
blank face is not
now so the dead
have nothing to go
by and are fast
or slow but never punctual
as the alarm is
over their bleached bones
of its night-strangled cry.

THE WAY OF IT

With her fingers she turns paint
into flowers, with her body
flowers into a remembrance
of herself. She is at work
always, mending the garment
of our marriage, foraging
like a bird for something
for us to eat. If there are thorns
in my life, it is she who
will press her breast to them and sing.

Her words, when she would scold,
are too sharp. She is busy
after for hours rubbing smiles
into the wounds. I saw her,
when young, and spread the panoply
of my feathers instinctively
to engage her. She was not deceived,
but accepted me as a girl
will under a thin moon
in love's absence as someone
she could build a home with
for her imagined child.

THE GAP

God woke, but the nightmare
did not recede. Word by word
the tower of speech grew.
He looked at it from the air
he reclined on. One word more and
it would be on a level
with him; vocabulary
would have triumphed. He

measured the thin gap
with his mind. No, no, no,
wider than that! But the nearness
persisted. How to live with
the fact, that was the feat
now. How to take his rest
on the edge of a chasm a
word could bridge.
                    He leaned
over and looked in the dictionary
they used. There was the blank still
by his name of the same
order as the territory
between them, the verbal hunger
for the thing in itself. And the darkness
that is a god's blood swelled
in him, and he let it
to make the sign in the space
on the page; that is in all languages
and none; that is the grammarian's
torment and the mystery
at the cell's core, and the equation
that will not come out, and is
the narrowness that we stare
over into the eternal
silence that is the repose of God.

PRESENT

I engage with philosophy
in the morning, with the garden
in the afternoon. Evenings I
fish or coming home empty-handed
put on the music of
César Franck. It is enough,
this. I would be the mirror

of a mirror, effortlessly repeating
my reflections. But there is that
one who will not leave me
alone, writing to me
of her fear; and the news from the city
is not good. I am at the switchboard
of the exchanges of the people
of all time, receiving their messages
whether I will or no. Do you
love me? the voices cry.
And there is no answer; there are
only the treaties and take-overs,
and the vision of clasped
hands over the unquiet blood.

THE PORCH

Do you want to know his name?
It is forgotten. Would you learn
what he was like? He was like
anyone else, a man with ears
and eyes. Be it sufficient
that in a church porch on an evening
in winter, the moon rising, the frost
sharp, he was driven
to his knees and for no reason
he knew. The cold came at him;
his breath was carved angularly
as the tombstones; an owl screamed.

He had no power to pray.
His back turned on the interior
he looked out on a universe
that was without knowledge
of him and kept his place
there for an hour on that lean
threshold, neither outside nor in.

GROPING

Moving away is only to the boundaries
of the self. Better to stay here,
I said, leaving the horizons
clear. The best journey to make
is inward. It is the interior
that calls. Eliot heard it.
Wordsworth turned from the great hills
of the north to the precipice
of his own mind, and let himself
down for the poetry stranded
on the bare ledges.
                            For some
it is all darkness; for me, too,
it is dark. But there are hands
there I can take, voices to hear
solider than the echoes
without. And sometimes a strange light
shines, purer than the moon,
casting no shadow, that is
the halo upon the bones
of the pioneers who died for truth.

THE WOMAN

So beautiful—God himself quailed
at her approach: the long body curved
like the horizon. Why had he made
her so? How would it be, she said,
leaning towards him, if, instead of
quarrelling over it, we divided it
between us? You can have all the credit
for its invention, if you will leave the ordering
of it to me. He looked into her
eyes and saw far down the bones
of the generations that would navigate

by those great stars, but the pull of it
was too much. Yes, he thought, give me their minds'
tribute, and what they do with their bodies
is not my concern. He put his hand in his side
and drew out the thorn for the letting
of the ordained blood and touched her with
it. Go, he said. They shall come to you for ever
with their desire, and you shall bleed for them in return.

AT IT

I think he sits at that strange table
of Eddington's, that is not a table
at all, but nodes and molecules
pushing against molecules
and nodes; and he writes there
in invisible handwriting the instructions
the genes follow. I imagine his
face that is more the face
of a clock, and the time told by it
is now, though Greece is referred
to and Egypt and empires
not yet begun.
        And I would have
things to say to this God
at the judgement, storming at him,
as Job stormed with the eloquence
of the abused heart. But there will be
no judgement other than the verdict
of his calculations, that abstruse
geometry that proceeds eternally
in the silence beyond right and wrong.

THE TRUCE

That they should not advance
beyond certain limits left—
accidentally?—undefined;
and that compensation be paid
by the other side. Meanwhile the
peasant—There are no peasants
in Wales, he said, holding
his liquor as a gentleman
should not—went up and down
his acre, rejecting the pot
of gold at the rainbow's
end in favour of earthier
values: the subsidies gradually
propagating themselves on the guilt
of an urban class.
                              Strenuous
times! Never all day
did the procession of popular
images through the farm
kitchens cease; it was tiring
watching. Such truce as was
called in the invisible
warfare between bad and
worse were where two half-truths
faced one another over
the body of an exhausted
nation, each one waiting for
the other to be proved wrong.

NIGHT SKY

What they are saying is
that there is life there, too;

that the universe is the size it is
to enable us to catch up.

They have gone on from the human;
that shining is a reflection
of their intelligence. Godhead
is the colonisation by mind

of untenanted space. It is its own
light, a statement beyond language
of conceptual truth. Every night
is a rinsing myself of the darkness

that is in my veins. I let the stars inject me
with fire, silent as it is far,
but certain in its cauterising
of my despair. I am a slow

traveller, but there is more than time
to arrive. Resting in the intervals
of my breathing, I pick up the signals
relayed to me from a periphery I comprehend.

THE SMALL COUNTRY

Did I confuse the categories?
Was I blind?
Was I afraid of hubris
in identifying this land
with the kingdom? Those stories
about the far journeys, when it was here
at my door; the object
of my contempt that became
the toad with the jewel in its head!
Was a population so small
enough to be called, too many
to be chosen? I called it
an old man, ignoring the April

message proclaiming: Behold,
I make all things new.

The dinosaurs have gone their way
into the dark. The time-span
of their human counterparts
is shortened; everything
on this shrinking planet favours the survival
of the small people, whose horizons
are large only because they are content to look at them
from their own hills.
                              I grow old,
bending to enter the promised
land that was here all the time,
happy to eat the bread that was baked
in the poets' oven, breaking my speech
from the perennial tree
of my people and holding it in my blind hand.

BRAVO!

Oh, I know it and don't
care. I know there is nothing in me
but cells and chromosomes
waiting to beget chromosomes
and cells. You could take me to pieces
and there would be no angel hard
by, wringing its hands over
the demolition of its temple.
I accept I'm predictable,
that of the thousands of choices
open to me the computer can calculate
the one I'll make. There is a woman
I know, who is the catalyst
of my conversions, who is
a mineral to dazzle. She will

grow old and her lovers will not
pardon her for it. I have made her
songs in the laboratory
of my understanding, explosives timed
to go off in the blandness of time's face.

PRE-CAMBRIAN

Here I think of the centuries,
six million of them, they say.
Yesterday a fine rain fell;
today the warmth has brought out the crowds.
After Christ, what? The molecules
are without redemption. My shadow
sunning itself on this stone
remembers the lava. Zeus looked down
on a brave world, but there was
no love there; the architecture
of their temples was less permanent
than these waves. Plato, Aristotle,
all those who furrowed the calmness
of their foreheads are responsible
for the bomb. I am charmed here
by the serenity of the reflections
in the sea's mirror. It is a window
as well. What I need
now is a faith to enable me to out-stare
the grinning faces of the inmates of its asylum,
the failed experiments God put away.

SHADOWS

I close my eyes.
The darkness implies your presence,
the shadow of your steep mind

on my world. I shiver in it.
It is not your light that
can blind us; it is the splendour
of your darkness.
                    And so I listen
instead and hear the language
of silence, the sentence
without an end. Is it I, then,
who am being addressed? A God's words
are for their own sake; we hear
at our peril. Many of us have gone
mad in the mastering
of your medium.
                    I will open
my eyes on a world where the problems
remain but our doctrines
protect us. The shadow of the bent cross
is warmer than yours. I see how the sinners
of history run in and out
at its dark doors and are not confounded.

ADJUSTMENTS

Never known as anything
but an absence, I dare not name him
as God. Yet the adjustments
are made. There is an unseen
power, whose sphere is the cell
and the electron. We never catch
him at work, but can only say,
coming suddenly upon an amendment,
that here he had been. To demolish
a mountain you move it stone by stone
like the Japanese. To make a new coat
of an old, you add to it gradually
thread by thread, so such change
as occurs is more difficult to detect.

Patiently with invisible structures
he builds, and as patiently
we must pray, surrendering the ordering
of the ingredients to a wisdom that
is beyond our own. We must change the mood
to the passive. Let the deaf men
be helped; in the silence that has come
upon them, let some influence
work so those closed porches
be opened once more. Let the bomb
swerve. Let the raised knife of the murderer
be somehow deflected. There are no
laws there other than the limits of
our understanding. Remembering rock
penetrated by the grass-blade, corrected
by water, we must ask rather
for the transformation of the will
to evil, for more loving
mutations, for the better ventilating
of the atmosphere of the closed mind.

THE GAME

It is the play of a being
who is not serious in
his conclusions. Take this
from that, he says, and there is everything
left. Look over the edge
of the universe and you see
your own face staring
at you back, as it does
in a pool. And we are forced
into the game, reluctant
contestants; though the mathematicians
are best at it. Never mind, they
say, whether it is there

or not, so long as our like
can use it. And we are shattered
by their deductions. There is
a series that is without
end, yet the rules are built
on the impossibility of
its existence. It is
how you play, we cry, scanning
the future for an account
of our perfomance. But the rewards
are there even so, and history
festers with the number of the recipients
of them, the handsome, the fortunate,
the well-fed; those who cheated this
being when he was not looking.

WAITING

Face to face? Ah, no
God; such language falsifies
the relation. Nor side by side,
nor near you, nor anywhere
in time and space.
                Say you were,
when I came, your name
vouching for you, ubiquitous
in its explanations. The
earth bore and they reaped:
God, they said, looking
in your direction. The wind
changed; over the drowned
body it was you
they spat at.
            Young
I pronounced you. Older
I still do, but seldomer

now, leaning far out
over an immense depth, letting
your name go and waiting,
somewhere between faith and doubt,
for the echoes of its arrival.

THE POSSESSION

He is a religious man.
How often I have heard him say,
looking around him with his worried eyes
at the emptiness: There must be something.

It is the same at night, when,
rising from his fused prayers,
he faces the illuminated city
above him: All that brightness, he thinks,

and nobody there! I am nothing
religious. All I have is a piece
of the universal mind that reflects
infinite darkness between points of light.

THE EMPTY CHURCH

They laid this stone trap
for him, enticing him with candles,
as though he would come like some huge moth
out of the darkness to beat there.
Ah, he had burned himself
before in the human flame
and escaped, leaving the reason
torn. He will not come any more

to our lure. Why, then, do I kneel still
striking my prayers on a stone

heart? Is it in hope one
of them will ignite yet and throw
on its illumined walls the shadow
of someone greater than I can understand?

IN GREAT WATERS

You are there also
at the foot of the precipice
of water that was too steep
for the drowned: their breath broke
and they fell. You have made an altar
out of the deck of the lost
trawler whose spars
are your cross. The sand crumbles
like bread; the wine is
the light quietly lying
in its own chalice. There is
a sacrament there more beauty
than terror whose ministrant
you are and the aisles are full
of the sea shapes coming to its celebration.

PERHAPS

His intellect was the clear mirror
he looked in and saw the machinery of God
assemble itself? It was one that reflected
the emptiness that was where God
should have been. The mind's tools had
no power convincingly to put him
together. Looking in that mirror was a journey
through hill mist where, the higher
one ascends, the poorer the visibility

becomes. It could have led to despair
but for the consciousness of a presence
behind him, whose breath clouding
that looking-glass proved that it was alive.
To learn to distrust the distrust
of feeling—this then was the next step
for the seeker? To suffer himself to be persuaded
of intentions in being other than the crossing
of a receding boundary which did not exist?
To yield to an unfelt pressure that, irresistible
in itself, had the character of everything
but coercion? To believe, looking up
into invisible eyes shielded against love's
glare, in the ubiquity of a vast concern?

ROGER BACON

He had strange dreams
    that were real
in which he saw God
      showing him an aperture
        of the horizon wherein
were flasks and test-tubes.
      And the rainbow
ended there not in a pot
    of gold, but in colours
that, dissected, had the ingredients of
    the death ray.

    Faces at the window
      of his mind
had the false understanding
of flowers, but their eyes pointed
      like arrows to
an imprisoning cell.
                Yet
he dreamed on in curves

and equations
with the smell of saltpetre
in his nostrils, and saw the hole
    in God's side that is the wound
    of knowledge and
thrust his hand in it and believed.

EMERGING

Well, I said, better to wait
for him on some peninsula
of the spirit. Surely for one
with patience he will happen by
once in a while. It was the heart
spoke. The mind, sceptical as always
of the anthropomorphisms
of the fancy, knew he must be put together
like a poem or a composition
in music, that what he conforms to
is art. A promontory is a bare
place; no God leans down
out of the air to take the hand
extended to him. The generations have
watched there
in vain. We are beginning to see
now it is matter is the scaffolding
of spirit; that the poem emerges
from morphemes and phonemes; that
as form in sculpture is the prisoner
of the hard rock, so in everyday life
it is the plain facts and natural happenings
that conceal God and reveal him to us
little by little under the mind's tooling.

AFTER JERICHO

There is an aggression of fact
to be resisted successfully
only in verse, that fights language
with its own tools. Smile, poet,

among the ruins of a vocabulary
you blew your trumpet against.
It was a conscript army; your words,
every one of them, are volunteers.

SYNOPSIS

Plato offered us little
the Aristotelians did not
take back. Later Spinoza
rationalised our approach;
we were taught that love
is an intellectual mode
of our being. Yet Hume questioned
the very existence of lover
of loved. The self he left us
with was what Kant
failed to transcend or Hegel
to dissolve: that grey subject
of dread that Søren Kierkegaard
depicted crossing its thousands
of fathoms; the beast that rages
through history; that presides smiling
at the councils of the positivists.

THE WHITE TIGER

It was beautiful as God
must be beautiful; glacial
eyes that had looked on
violence and come to terms

with it; a body too huge
and majestic for the cage in which
it had been put; up
and down in the shadow

of its own bulk it went,
lifting, as it turned,
the crumpled flower of its face
to look into my own

face without seeing me. It
was the colour of the moonlight
on snow and as quiet
as moonlight, but breathing

as you can imagine that God
breathes within the confines
of our definition of him, agonising
over immensities that will not return.

THE ANSWER

Not darkness but twilight
in which even the best
of minds must make its way
now. And slowly the questions
occur, vague but formidable
for all that. We pass our hands
over their surface like blind
men, feeling for the mechanism
that will swing them aside. They

yield, but only to re-form
as new problems; and one
does not even do that
but towers immovable
before us.
                    Is there no way
other than thought of answering
its challenge? There is an anticipation
of it to the point of
dying. There have been times
when, after long on my knees
in a cold chancel, a stone has rolled
from my mind, and I have looked
in and seen the old questions lie
folded and in a place
by themselves, like the piled
graveclothes of love's risen body.

THE FILM OF GOD

Sound, too? The recorder
that picks up everything picked
up nothing but the natural
background. What language
does the god speak? And the camera's
lens, as sensitive to
an absence as to a presence,
saw what? What is the colour
of his thought?
                    It was blank, then,
the screen, as far as he
was concerned? It was a bare
landscape and harsh, and geological
its time. But the rock was
bright, the illuminated manuscript
of the lichen. And a shadow,

as we watched, fell, as though
of an unseen writer bending over
his work.
        It was not cloud
because it was not cold,
and dark only from the candlepower
behind it. And we waited
for it to move, silently
as the spool turned, waited
for the figure that cast it
to come into view for us to
identify it, and it
didn't and we are still waiting.

THE ABSENCE

It is this great absence
that is like a presence, that compels
me to address it without hope
of a reply. It is a room I enter

from which someone has just
gone, the vestibule for the arrival
of one who has not yet come.
I modernise the anachronism

of my language, but he is no more here
than before. Genes and molecules
have no more power to call
him up than the incense of the Hebrews

at their altars. My equations fail
as my words do. What resource have I
other than the emptiness without him of my whole
being, a vacuum he may not abhor?

EPIPHANY

Three kings? Not even one
any more. Royalty
has gone to ground, its journeyings
over. Who now will bring

gifts and to what place? In
the manger there are only the toys
and the tinsel. The child
has become a man. Far

off from his cross in the wrong
season he sits at table
with us with on his head
the fool's cap of our paper money.

PILGRIMAGES

There is an island there is no going
to but in a small boat the way
the saints went, travelling the gallery
of the frightened faces of
the long-drowned, munching the gravel
of its beaches. So I have gone
up the salt lane to the building
with the stone altar and the candles
gone out, and kneeled and lifted
my eyes to the furious gargoyle
of the owl that is like a god
gone small and resentful. There
is no body in the stained window
of the sky now. Am I too late?
Were they too late also, those
first pilgrims? He is such a fast
God, always before us and
leaving as we arrive.

                              There are those here
not given to prayer, whose office
is the blank sea that they say daily.
What they listen to is not
hymns but the slow chemistry of the soil
that turns saints' bones to dust,
dust to an irritant of the nostril.

There is no time on this island.
The swinging pendulum of the tide
has no clock; the events
are dateless. These people are not
late or soon; they are just
here with only the one question
to ask, which life answers
by being in them. It is I
who ask. Was the pilgrimage
I made to come to my own
self, to learn that in times
like these and for one like me
God will never be plain and
out there, but dark rather and
inexplicable, as though he were in here?

MONET: ROUEN CATHEDRAL, FULL SUNSHINE

But deep inside
are the chipped figures
with their budgerigar faces,
a sort of divine
humour in collusion
with time. Who but
God can improve
by distortion?

                There is
a stone twittering in
the cathedral branches,
the excitement of migrants
newly arrived from a tremendous
presence.
                We have no food
for them but our
prayers. Kneeling we drop our
crumbs, apologising
for their dryness, afraid
to look up in the ensuing
silence in case they have flown.

RENOIR: THE BATHERS

What do they say?
    Here is flesh
not to be peeped
    at. No Godivas
these. They remain
    not pass, naked
for us to gaze
    our fill on, but
without lust.
                This
    is the mind's feast,
where taste follows
    participation. Values
are in reverse
    here. Such soft tones
are for the eye
    only. These bodies,
smooth as bells
    from art's stroking, toll
an unheard music,

keep such firmness
of line as never,
   under the lapping
of all this light
   to become blurred or dim.

DIRECTIONS

In this desert of language
   we find ourselves in,
with the sign-post with the word 'God'
   worn away
   and the distance. . . . ?

Pity the simpleton
   with his mouth open crying:
            How far is it to God?

And the wiseacre says: Where you were,
friend.
      You know that smile
                     glossy
as the machine that thinks it has outpaced
   belief?
            I am one of those
who sees from the arms opened
            to embrace the future
the shadow of the Cross fall
   on the smoothest of surfaces
            causing me to stumble.

COVENANT

I feel sometimes
   we are his penance

for having made us. He
suffers in us and we partake
        of his suffering. What
to do, when it has been done
        already? Where
        to go, when the arrival
is as the departure? Circularity
is a mental condition, the
animals know nothing of it.

        Seven times have passed
over him, and he is still here.
        When will he return
from his human exile, and will
peace then be restored
        to the flesh?
                        Often
I think that there is no end
to this torment and that the electricity
that convulses us is the fire
        in which a god
burns and is not consumed.

WAITING FOR IT

Yeats said that. Young
I delighted in it:
there was time enough.

Fingers burned, heart
seared, a bad taste
in the mouth, I read him

again, but without trust
any more. What counsel
has the pen's rhetoric

to impart? Break mirrors, stare
ghosts in the face, try
walking without crutches

at the grave's edge? Now
in the small hours
of belief the one eloquence

to master is that
of the bowed head, the bent
knee, waiting, as at the end

of a hard winter
for one flower to open
on the mind's tree of thorns.

CORRESPONDENCE

You ask why I don't write.
But what is there to say?
The salt current swings in and out
of the bay, as it has done
time out of mind. How does that help?
It leaves illegible writing
on the shore. If you were here,
we would quarrel about it.
People file past this seascape
as ignorantly as through a gallery
of great art. I keep searching for meaning.
The waves are a moving staircase
to climb, but in thought only.
The fall from the top is as sheer
as ever. Younger I deemed truth
was to come at beyond the horizon.
Older I stay still and am
as far off as before. These nail-parings
bore you? They explain my silence.

I wish there were as simple
an explanation for the silence of God.

AIE!

The flowers of childhood
are fadeless and have
a sweet smell. Our hearts are
vases, standing in the window

that looks out on to Eden's
garden. But our minds
are of glass also and
refrigerate us with a different view.

PLUPERFECT

It was because there was nothing to do
that I did it; because silence was golden
I broke it. There was a vacuum
I found myself in, full of echoes
of dead languages. Where to turn
when there are no corners? In curved
space I kept on arriving
at my departures. I left no stones
unraised, but always wings
were tardy to start. In ante-rooms
of the spirit I suffered the anaesthetic
of time and came to with my hurt
unmended. Where are you? I
shouted, growing old in
the interval between here and now.

FAIR DAY

They come in from the fields
with the dew and the buttercup dust
on their boots. It was not they
nor their ancestors crucified
Christ. They look up at what
the town has done to him,
hanging his body in stone on a stone
cross, as though to commemorate
the bringing of the divine beast
to bay and disabling him.

He is hung up high, but higher
are the cranes and scaffolding
of the future. And they stand by,
men from the past, whose rôle
is to assist in the destruction
of the past, bringing their own beasts
in to offer their blood up
on a shoddier altar.
                                 The town
is malignant. It grows, and what
it feeds on is what these men call
their home. Is there praise
here? There is the noise of those
buying and selling and mortgaging
their conscience, while the stone
eyes look down tearlessly. There
is not even anger in them any more.

VOICES

Who to believe?
The linnet sings bell-like,

a tinkling music. It says life
is contained here; is a jewel

in a shell casket, lying
among down. There is another
voice, far out in space,
whose persuasiveness is the distance

from which it speaks. Divided
mind, the message is always
in two parts. Must it be
on a cross it is made one?

ALEPH

What is time? The man stands
in the grass under
the willow by the grey
water corrugated
by wind, and his spirit reminds
him of how it was always
so, in Athens, in Sumer under
the great king. The moment
is history's navel
and round it the worlds
spin. Was there desire
in the past? It is fulfilled
here. The mind has emerged
from the long cave without
looking back, leading eternity
by the hand, and together they pause
on the adult threshold
recuperating endlessly
in intermissions of the machine.

SEVENTIETH BIRTHDAY

Made of tissue and H$_2$O,
and activated by cells
firing—Ah, heart, the legend
of your person! Did I invent
it, and is it in being still?

In the competition with other
women your victory is assured.
It is time, as Yeats said, is
the caterpillar in the cheek's rose,
the untiring witherer of your petals.

You are drifting away from
me on the whitening current of your hair.
I lean far out from the bone's bough,
knowing the hand I extend
can save nothing of you but your love.

ONE WAY

There was a frontier
I crossed whose passport
was human speech. Looking back
was to silence, to that
wood of hands fumbling
for the unseen thing. I
named it and it was
here. I held out words
to them and they smelled
them. Space gave, time was
eroded. There was one being
would not reply. God,
I whispered, refining
my technique, signalling
to him on the frequencies

I commanded. But always
amid the air's garrulousness
there was one station
that remained closed.
                              Was
there an alternative
medium? There were some claimed
to be able to call him
down to drink insatiably
at the dark sumps of blood.

MEDITERRANEAN

The water is the same;
it is the reflections are different.
Virgil looked in this
mirror. You would not think so.

The lights' jewellery sticks in the throat
of the fish; open
them, you will find a debased
coinage to pay your taxes.

The cicadas sing
on. Looking for them among
the ilex is like trying to translate
a poem into another language.

CODE

He grew up into an emptiness
he was on terms with. The duplicity
of language, that could name
what was not there, was accepted

by him. He was content, remembering
the unseen writing of Christ
on the ground, to interpret
it in his own way. Adultery

of the flesh has the divine
pardon. It is the mind,
catching itself in the act
of unfaithfulness, that must cast no stone.

SENIOR

At sixty there are still fables
to outgrow, the possessiveness
of language. There is no book
of life with the pen ready
to delete one's name. Judgment
days are the trials we attend
here, whose verdict the future
has no interest in. Is there
a sentence without words?
                                    God
is a mode of prayer; cease
speaking and there is only
the silence. Has he his own
media of communication?

What is a galaxy's meaning?
The stars relay to the waste
places of the earth, as they do
to the towns, but it is
a cold message. There is randomness
at the centre, agitation subsisting
at the heart of what would be
endless peace.
                    A man's shadow
falls upon rocks that are

millions of years old, and
thought comes to drink at that dark
pool, but goes away thirsty.

THE NEW MARINER

In the silence
that is his chosen medium
of communication and telling
others about it
in words. Is there no way
not to be the sport
of reason? For me now
there is only the God-space
into which I send out
my probes. I had looked forward
to old age as a time
of quietness, a time to draw
my horizons about me,
to watch memories ripening
in the sunlight of a walled garden.
But there is the void
over my head and the distance
within that the tireless signals
come from. And astronaut
on impossible journeys
to the far side of the self
I return with messages
I cannot decipher, garrulous
about them, worrying the ear
of the passer-by, hot on his way
to the marriage of plain fact with plain fact.

BEACONS

Whose address was the corridors
of Europe, waiting for the summons
to be interrogated on their lack of guilt.

Their flesh was dough for the hot
ovens. Some of them rose
to the occasion. The nerves of some

were instruments on which the guards fingered
obscene music. Were there prayers
said? Did a god hear? Time heard

them, anticipating their requital.
Their wrong is an echo defying
acoustical law, increasing not fading.

Evil's crumbling anonymity
is at an end now. We recognise
it by the eternal phosphorous

of their bones, and make our way on
by that same light to the birth
of an innocence that is curled up in the will.

BENT

Heads bowed
    over the entrails,
over the manuscript, the
block, over the rows
            of swedes.

Do they never look up?
    Why should one think
that to be on one's knees
    is to pray?

The aim is to walk tall
        in the sun.
Did the weight of the jaw
    bend their backs,
keeping their vision
    below the horizon?

Two million years
in straightening them
    out, and they are still bent
over the charts, the instruments,
            the drawing-board,
the mathematical navel
    that is the wink of God.

FLOWERS

But behind the flower
is that other flower
which is ageless, the idea
of the flower, the one
we smell when we imagine
it, that as often
as it is picked blossoms
again, that has the perfection
of all flowers, the purity
without the fragility.
                    Was it
a part of the plan
for humanity to have
flowers about it? They are many
and beautiful, with faces
that are a reminder of those
of our own children, though they come painlessly
from the bulb's womb. We trouble
them as we go by, so they hang

their heads at our unreal
progress.
             If flowers had minds,
would they not think they were the colour
eternity is, a window that gives
on a still view the hurrying
people must come to and stare at and pass by?

MINOR

Nietzsche had a word
for it. History discredits
his language. Ours
more quietly rusts

in autumnal libraries
of the spirit. Scolded
for small faults,
we see how violence in others

is secretly respected.
Do we amble pacifically
towards our extinction? The answers
from over the water

are blood-red. I wonder,
seeing the rock
split by green grass
as efficiently

as the atom, is this
the centre from which
nature will watch out
human folly, until

it is time to call back
to the small field civilisation
began in the small
people the giants deposed?

OBSERVATION

Recalling adventures:
One person, he thinks,
in every century or so
came within hail.
I answered by standing
aside, watching him
as he passed. I
am the eternal quarry,
moving at thought's
speed, following
the hunger, arriving
before him. They
put down their prayers'
bait, and swallow it
themselves. Somewhere
between word and deed
are the equations
I step over. Why
do they stare out
with appalled minds
at the appetite
of their lenses?
It is where I feed,
too, waiting for them
to catch up, bounded
only by an inability
to be overtaken.

PATTERNS

The old men ask
for more time, while the young
waste it. And the philosopher
smiles, knowing there is none

there. But the hero stands
sword drawn at the looking-glass
of his mind, aiming at that
anonymous face over his shoulder.

THE PRESENCE

I pray and incur
silence. Some take that silence
for refusal.
            I feel the power
that, invisible, catches me
by the sleeve, nudging
            towards the long shelf
that has the book on it I will take down
            and read and find the antidote
to an ailment.
            I know its ways with me;
how it enters my life,
            is present rather
before I perceive it, sunlight quivering
on a bare wall.
            Is it consciousness trying
to get through?
            Am I under
regard?
            It takes me seconds
to focus, by which time
            it has shifted its gaze,
looking a little to one
            side, as though I were not here.

It has the universe
            to be abroad in.
There is nothing I can do
but fill myself with my own

silence, hoping it will approach
like a wild creature to drink
there, or perhaps like Narcissus
to linger a moment over its transparent face.

FOREST DWELLERS

Men who have hardly uncurled
from their posture in the
womb. Naked. Heads bowed, not
in prayer, but in contemplation
of the earth they came from,
that suckled them on the brown
milk that builds bone not brain.

Who called them forth to walk
in the green light, their thoughts
on darkness? Their women,
who are not Madonnas, have babes
at the breast with the wise,
time-ridden faces of the Christ
child in a painting by a Florentine

master. The warriors prepare poison
with love's care for the Sebastians
of their arrows. They have no
God, but follow the contradictions
of a ritual that says
life must die that life
may go on. They wear flowers in their hair.

RETURN

Taking the next train
to the city, yet always returning

to his place on a bridge
over a river, throbbing

with trout, whose widening
circles are the mandala
for contentment. So will a poet
return to the work laid

on one side and abandoned
for the voices summoning him
to the wrong tasks. Art
is not life. It is not the river

carrying us away, but the motionless
image of itself on a fast-
running surface with which life
tries constantly to keep up.

THRESHOLD

I emerge from the mind's
cave into the worse darkness
outside, where things pass and
the Lord is in none of them.

I have heard the still, small voice
and it was that of the bacteria
demolishing my cosmos. I
have lingered too long on

this threshold, but where can I go?
To look back is to lose the soul
I was leading upwards towards
the light. To look forward? Ah,

what balance is needed at
the edges of such an abyss.
I am alone on the surface
of a turning planet. What

to do but, like Michelangelo's
Adam, put my hand
out into unknown space,
hoping for the reciprocating touch?

SALT

The centuries were without
his like; then suddenly
he was there, fishing
in a hurrying river,
the Teifi. But what he caught
were ideas; the water
described a direction;
his thoughts were toy boats
that grew big; one
he embarked on: Suez,
the Far East—the atlas
became familiar
to him as a back-yard.

'Spittle and phlegm!
Listen, sailor,
to the wind piping
in the thin rigging;
go climbing there
to the empty nest
of the black crow. Far
is the deck and farther
your courage.'
                    'Captain,
captain, long
is the wind's tongue
and cold your porridge.
Look up now
and dry your beard;

teach me to ride
in my high saddle
the mare of the sea.'
He fell.
Was it the fall
of the soul
from favour? Past four
decks, and his bones
splintered. Seventeen weeks
on his back. No Welsh,
no English; but the hands
of the Romanians
kind. He became
their mouth-piece, publishing
his rebirth. In a new
body he sailed
away on his old course.

On brisk evenings
before the Trades
the sails named
themselves; he repeated
the lesson. The First
Mate had a hard boot.

Cassiopeia, Sirius,
all the stars
over him, yet none of them
with a Welsh sound.
But the capstan spoke
in *cynghanedd*; from
breaker to breaker
he neared home.

'Evening, sailor.' Red
lips and tilted smile;
the ports garlanded
with faces. Was he aware
of a vicarage garden

that was the cramped harbour
he came to?
                    Later
the letters began: 'Dear—'
the small pen
in the stubbed hand—
'in these dark waters
the memory of you
is like a—' words scratched
out that would win a smile
from the reader. The deep
sea and the old call
to abandon it
for the narrow channel
from her and back. The chair
was waiting and the slippers
by the soft fire
that would destroy him.

'The hard love I had at her small breasts;
the tight fists that pummelled me;
the thin mouth with its teeth clenched
on a memory.' Are all women
like this? He said so, that man,
my father, who had tasted their lips'
vinegar, coughing it up
in harbours he returned to with his tongue
lolling from droughts of the sea.

The voice of my father
in the night with the hunger
of the sea in it and the emptiness
of the sea. While the house founders
in time, I must listen to him
complaining, a ship's captain
with no crew, a navigator
without a port; rejected
by the barrenness of his wife's
coasts, by the wind's bitterness

off her heart. I take his failure
for ensign, flying it
at my bedpost, where my own
children cry to be born.

Suddenly he was old
in a silence unhaunted
by the wailing signals;

and was put ashore
on that four-walled
island to which all sailors must come.

So he went gleaning
in the flickering stubble,
where formerly his keel reaped.

And the remembered stars
swarmed for him; and the birds, too,
most of them with wrong names.

Always he looked aft
from the chair's bridge, and his hearers
suffered the anachronism of his view.

The form of his
life; the weak smile;
the fingers filed down
by canvas; the hopes
blunted; the lack of understanding
of life creasing the brow
with wrinkles, as though he pondered
on deep things.
                    Out of touch
with the times, landlocked
in his ears' calm, he remembered
and talked; spoiling himself
with his mirth; running the joke
down; giving his orders
again in hospital with his crew
gone. What was a sailor

good for who had sailed
all seas and learned wisdom
from none, fetched up there
in the shallows with his mind's
valueless cargo?

Strange grace, sailor, docked now
in six feet of thick soil,
with the light dribbling on you
from the lamps in a street
of a town you had no love
for. The place is a harbour
for stone sails, and under
it you lie with the becalmed
fleet heavy upon you. This
was never the destination
you dreamed of in that other
churchyard by Teifi.
              And I,
can I accept your voyages
are done; that there is no tide
high enough to float you off
this mean shoal of plastic
and trash? Six feet down,
and the bone's anchor too
heavy for your child spirit
to haul on and be up and away?

PLAS DIFANCOLL

I

Trees, of course, silent attendants,
though no more silent than footmen
at the great table, ministering shadows
waiting only to be ignored.

Leaves of glass, full of the year's
wine, broken repeatedly and
as repeatedly replaced.
A garden ventilated by cool

fountains. Two huge lions
of stone, rampant at the drive
gates, intimidating no-one
but those lately arrived

and wondering whether they are too early.
Between hillsides the large house,
classical and out of place
in the landscape, as Welsh as

it is unpronounceable. He
and she, magnificent both, not least
in the confidence of their ignorance
of the insubordination of the future.

2

Down to two servants now and those
grown cheeky; unvisited any more

by the county. The rust of autumn
outside on the landscape and inside in the joints

of these hangers-on. Time running out
for them here in the broken hour-glass

that they live in with its cracked
windows mirroring a consumptive moon.

The fish starve in their waters or
are pilfered from them by the unpunished trespassers

from far away. The place leans on itself,
sags. There is a conspiracy of the ivy

to bring it down, with no prayers
going up from the meeting-house for its salvation.

3

The owls' home and the starlings',
with moss bandaging its deep wounds
to no purpose, for the wind festers in
them and the light diagnoses
impartially the hopelessness
of its condition. Colonialism
is a lost cause. Yet the Welsh
are here, picknicking among the ruins
on their Corona and potato
crisps, speaking their language without pride,
but with no backward look over their shoulder.

PERSPECTIVES

Primeval

Beasts rearing from green slime—
an illiterate country, unable to read
its own name. Stones moved into position
on the hills' sides; snakes laid their eggs
in their cold shadow. The earth suffered
the sky's shrapnel, bled yellow
into the enraged sea. At night heavily
over the heaving forests the moon
sagged. The ancestors of the tigers
brightened their claws. Such sounds
as there were came from the strong
torn by the stronger. The dawn tilted
an unpolished mirror for the runt mind
to look at itself in without recognition.

Neolithic

I shall not be here,
and the way things are going

now won't want to be.
Wheels go no faster
than what pulls them. That land
visible over the sea
in clear weather, they say
we will get there some time
soon and take possession
of it. What then? More acres
to cultivate and no markets
for the crops.
                    The young
are not what they were,
smirking at the auspices
of the entrails. Some think
there will be a revival.
I don't believe it. This
plucked music has come
to stay. The natural breathing
of the pipes was to
a different god. Imagine
depending on the intestines
of a polecat for accompaniment
to one's worship! I have
attended at the sacrifice
of the language that is the liturgy
the priests like, and felt
the draught that was God
leaving. I think some day
there will be nothing left
but to go back to the place
I came from and wrap
myself in the memory
of how I was young
once and under the covenant
of that God not given to folly.

Christian

They were bearded
like the sea they came
from; rang stone bells
for their stone hearers.

Their cells fitted them
like a coffin.
Out of them their prayers
seeped, delicate

flowers where weeds
grew. Their dry bread
broke like a bone.
Wine in the cup

was a blood-stained mirror
for sinners to look
into with one eye
closed, and see themselves forgiven.

Mediaeval

I was my lord's bard,
telling again sweetly
what had been done bloodily.

We lived in a valley;
he had no lady.
Fame was our horizon.

In the spring of the year
the wind brought the news
of a woman's beauty.

Her eyes were still stones
in her smooth-running hair.
Her voice was the birds' envy.

We made a brave foray;
the engagement was furious.
We came back alone.

158

Sing me, my lord said,
the things nearer home:
my falcons, my horse.

I did so, he listened.
My harp was of fire;
the notes bounced like sparks

off his spirit's anvil.
To-morrow, he promised,
we will ride forth again.

Modern

And the brittle gardens
of Dinorwig, deep
in the fallen petals of
their slate flowers: such the autumn

of a people! Whose spring
is it sleeps in a glass
bulb, ready to astonish us
with its brilliance? Bring

on the dancing girls
of the future, the swaying
pylons with their metal
hair bickering towards England.

COVENANTERS

Jesus

He wore no hat, but he produced, say
from up his sleeve, an answer
to their question about
the next life. It is here,
he said, tapping his forehead
as one would to indicate
an idiot. The crowd frowned

and took up stones
to punish his adultery
with the truth. But he, stooping
to write on the ground, looked
sideways at them, as they withdrew
each to the glass-house of his own mind.

Mary

Model of models;
virgin smile over
the ageless babe,

my portrait is in
the world's galleries:
motherhood without

a husband; chastity
my complexion. Cradle
of flesh for one

not born of the flesh.
Alas, you painters
of a half-truth, the

poets excel you.
They looked in under
my lids and saw

as through a stained glass
window the hill
the infant must climb,

the crookedness of
the kiss he appended
to his loving epistle.

Joseph

I knew what I knew.
She denied it.
I went with her

on the long journey.
My seed, was the star
that the wise men
followed. Their gifts were no good
to us. I taught him
the true trade: to go
with the grain.
            He left me
for a new master
who put him to the fashioning
of a cross for himself.

Lazarus

That imperious summons! Spring's
restlessness among dry
leaves. He stands at the grave's
entrance and rubs death from his eyes,

while thought's fountain recommences
its play, watering the waste ground
over again for the germination
of the blood's seed, where roses should blow.

Judas Iscariot

picked flowers stole birds' eggs
like the rest was his mother's
fondling passed under the tree
he would hang from without
realising looked through the branches
saw only the cloud face
of God and the sky mirroring
the water he was brought up by

was a shrewd youth with a talent
for sums became treasurer
to the disciplines was genuinely
hurt by a certain extravagance

in the Master went out of his own
free will to do that which he had to do.

Paul

Wrong question, Paul. Who am I,
Lord? is what you should have asked.
And the answer, surely, somebody
who it is easy for us to kick against.
There were some matters you were dead right
about. For instance, I like you
on love. But marriage—I could have thought
too many had been burned in that fire
for your contrast to hold.

                    Still, you are the mountain
the teaching of the carpenter of Nazareth
congealed into. The theologians
have walked around you for centuries
and none of them scaled you. Your letters remain
unanswered, but survive the recipients
of them. And we, pottering among the foot-hills
of their logic, find ourselves staring
across deep crevices at conclusions at which
the living Jesus would not willingly have arrived.

THIRTEEN BLACKBIRDS LOOK AT A MAN

I

It is calm.
It is as though
we lived in a garden
that had not yet arrived
at the knowledge of
good and evil.
But there is a man in it.

2

There will be
rain falling vertically
from an indifferent
sky. There will stare out
from behind its
bars the face of the man
who is not enjoying it.

3

Nothing higher
than a blackberry
bush. As the sun comes up
fresh, what is the darkness
stretching from horizon
to horizon? It is the shadow
here of the forked man.

4

We have eaten
the blackberries and spat out
the seeds, but they lie
glittering like the eyes of a man.

5

After we have stopped
singing, the garden is disturbed
by echoes; it is
the man whistling, expecting
everything to come to him.

6

We wipe our beaks
on the branches
wasting the dawn's

jewellery to get rid
of the taste of a man.

7

Nevertheless,
which is not the case
with a man, our
bills give us no trouble.

8

Who said the
number was unlucky?
It was a man, who,
trying to pass us,
had his licence endorsed
thirteen times.

9

In the cool
of the day the garden
seems given over
to blackbirds. Yet
we know also that somewhere
there is a man in hiding.

10

To us there are
eggs and there are
blackbirds. But there is the man,
too, trying without feathers
to incubate a solution.

11

We spread our
wings, reticulating

our air-space. A man stands
under us and worries
at his ability to do the same.

12

When night comes
like a visitor
from outer space
we stop our ears
lest we should hear tell
of the man in the moon.

13

Summer is
at an end. The migrants
depart. When they return
in spring to the garden,
will there be a man among them?

ADAGIO

Conversations between glass.
    Time weep for us.
I weep for time never
soon enough to anticipate
a reflection.
        The poet stands
beneath leafless trees
        listening to the wind
bowing on their wires. What
it affirms is: The way on
    is over your shoulder;
you must lean forward
to look back. No rhymes
        needed for such verse.

They have moved a little nearer
the light to accentuate
    their shadows, white-collared
    men at their dark trades.
Their laboratories shine
        with a cold radiance,
leprosy to me who have watched them run
    through the corridors of our culture
shaking the carillon
    of their instruments at us
        and crying: Unclean!

GRADUAL

I have come to the borders
of the understanding. Instruct
me, God, whether to press
onward or to draw back.

To say I am a child
is a pretence at humility
that is unworthy of me.
Rather am I at one with those

minds, all of whose instruments
are beside the point of
their sharpness. I need a technique
other than that of physics

for registering the ubiquity
of your presence. A myriad prayers
are addressed to you in a thousand
languages and you decode

them all. Liberty for you
is freedom from our too human
senses, yet we die
when they nod. Call your horizons

in. Suffer the domestication
for a moment of the ferocities
you inhabit, a garden for us to refine
our ignorance in under the boughs of love.

MEASURE FOR MEASURE

In every corner
        of the dark triangle
sex spins its web; the characters
are ensnared; virtue
is its own undoing, lust posing
        as love. Life's innocent
need of itself is the prime sin.

And no-one able to explain why
at the margins of her habit
the fifteenth phase of the flesh
        so mercilessly dazzles.

THE OTHER

They did it to me.
I preferred dead, lying
in the mind's mortuary.
Come out, they shouted;
with a screech of steel
I jumped into the world
smiling my cogged smile,
breaking with iron hand
the hands they extended.

They rose in revolt;
I cropped them like tall
grass; munched on the cud

of nations. A little oil,
I begged in conspiracy
with disaster. Ice
in your veins, the poet
taunted; the life in you
ticking away; your breath
poison. I took him apart
verse by verse, turning
on him my x-ray
eyes to expose the emptiness
of his interiors. In houses
with no hearth he huddles
against me now, mortgaging
his dwindling techniques
for the amenities I offer.

STRAYS

Of all the women of the fields—
      full skirt, small waist—
the scarecrow is the best dressed.

She has an air about her
      which more than makes up
for her loss of face.

There is nothing between us.
      If I take her arm
there is nowhere to go.

We are alone and strollers
      of a fine day with
under us the earth's fathoms waiting.

IT

We agreed
it was terrible.
One with a gift
of words multiplied
comparisons, as when two
mirrors reflect one another.
It remained unique.
Sometimes awaking
in moonlight, I imagined
it chemically composed.
But beyond was the dark
seeping from it as from a split mind.
Was it a nervous system
with stars firing
at the synapses? It had no
place, yet the thought came
that if it should move
we would burn or freeze.
The scientists breach
themselves with their Caesarian
births, and we blame them for it.
What shall we do
with the knowledge growing
into a tree that to shelter
under is to be lightning struck?

THE CONES

But why a thousand? I ask.
It is like breaking off
a flake from the great pyramid
of time and exalting the molecules
into wholes. The pyramid
is the hive to which

generation after generation
comes with nectar for the making
of the honey it shall not eat.
Emperors and their queens? Pollen
blown away from forgotten
flowers. Wars? Scratches upon earth's
ageless face. He leads us to expect
too much. Following his star,
we will find in the manger
as the millenium dies neither
the child reborn nor the execrable
monster, but only the curled-up
doll, whose spring is the tribute
we bring it, that before we have done
rubbing our eyes will be back
once more in the arms of the maternal
grass in travesty of the Pietà.

ADDER

What is this creature discarded
like a toy necklace
among the weeds and flowers,
singing to me silently

of the fire never to be put out
at its thin lips? It is scion
of a mighty ancestor
that spoke the language

of trees to our first
parents and greened its scales
in the forbidden one, timelessly shining
as though autumn were never to be.

CADENZA

Is absence enough?
I asked from my absent place
by love's fire. What god,
fingers in its ears, leered at me
from above the lintel, face
worn by the lapping
of too much time? Leaves prompted
to prayer, green hands folded
in green evenings. Who
to? I questioned, avoiding
that chipped gaze. Was lightning
the answer, scissoring
between clouds, the divine
cut-out with his veins
on fire? That such brightness
should be attended by such
noise! I supposed, watching
the starry equations,
his thinking was done
in a great silence; yet after
he goes out, following
himself into oblivion,
the memory of him must smoke
on in this ash, waiting
for the believing people
to blow on it. So some say
were the stars born. So,
say I, are those sparks
forged that are knocked like nails
one by one into the usurping flesh.

CENTURIES

The fifteenth passes with drums and in armour;
the monk watches it through the mind's grating.

The sixteenth puts on its cap and bells
to poach vocabulary from a king's laughter.

The seventeenth wears a collar of lace
at its neck, the flesh running from thought's candle.

The eighteenth has a high fever and hot blood,
but clears its nostrils with the snuff of wit.

The nineteenth emerges from history's cave
rubbing its eyes at the glass prospect.

The twentieth is what is looked forward to
beating its wings at windows that are not there.

THE TREE

So God is born
        from our loss of nerve?
He is the tree that looms up
in our darkness, at whose feet
we must fall to be set again
on its branches on some April day
of the heart.
            He needs us
as a conductor his choir
for the performance of an unending
music.
        What we may not
do is to have our horizon bare,
        is to make our way
on through a desert white with the bones
of our dead faiths. It is why,

some say, if there were no tree,
we would have to set one up
            for us to linger under,
its drops falling on us as though to confirm
he has blood like ourselves.
We have set one up, but
of steel and so leafless that
            he has taken himself
off out of the reach
of our transmitted prayers.
                            Nightly
we explore the universe
on our wave-lengths, picking up nothing
            but those acoustic ghosts
that could as well be mineral
            signalling mineral
as immortal mind communicating with itself.

THE VOW

The supreme vow is no
vow but a concession
to anger at the exigencies
of language. The hero

is he who advances
with all his vocabulary
intact to his final
overthrow by an untruth.

GRANDPARENTS

With the deterioration of sight
they see more clearly what is missing

from their expressions. With the
dulling of the ear, the silences
before the endearments are
louder than ever. Their hands have their accidents
still, but no hospital will
receive them. With their licences
expired, though they keep to their own
side, there are corners
in waiting. Theirs is a strange
house. Over the door in
invisible letters there is the name:
Home, but it is no place
to return to. On the floor
are the upset smiles, on the
table the cups unwashed they drank
their happiness from. There are themselves
at the windows, faces staring
at an unreached finishing
post. There is the sound
in the silence of the breathing
of their reluctant bodies as
they enter each of them the last lap.

PUBLICITY INC.

Homo sapiens to the Creator:
Greetings, on the mind's kiloherz.
For yours of no date,
thanks. This is to advise
that as of now our address
broadens to include the planets
and the intervals between. No
longer the old gravitational
pull. We are as much
out there as down here. As likely
to meet you on the way back

as at our departure.
You refer to the fading away
of our prayers. May we suggest
you try listening on the inter-galactic
channel? Realising the sound
returned to us from a flower's
speaking-trumpet was an echo
of our own voices, we have switched
our praise, directing it rather
at those mysterious sources
of the imagination you yourself
drink from, metabolising
them instantly in space-time
to become the ichor of your radiation.

HISTORY

It appears before us,
        wringing its dry hands,
quoting from Nietzsche's book,
        from Schopenhauer.

Sing us, we say,
        more sunlit occasions;
the child by the still pool
        multiplying reflections.

It remains unconsoled
        in its dust-storm of tears,
remembering the Crusades,
        the tortures, the purges.

But time passes by;
        it commits adultery
with it to father the cause
        of its continued weeping.

PASSAGE

I was Shakespeare's man that time,
        walking under a waned moon
to hear the barn owl cry:
        Treason. My sword failed me,
            withering at its green
tip.
        I took Donne's word,
clothing my thought's skeleton
        in black lace, walking awhile
        by the bone's light;
but the tombstone misled me.

        Shelley put forth
his waxwork hand, that came off
in my own and I sank down
        with him to see time
        at its experiment at the sand's
table.
        I walked Yeats'
street, pausing at the flowering
        of the water in a shop
window, foreseeing its drooping
        from being too often
smelled.
        I stand now, tolling my name
in the poem's empty church,
        summoning to the celebration
        at which the transplanted
organs are loth to arrive.

QUESTIONS

Prepare yourself for the message.
You are prepared?
                    Silence.
Silence is the message.
The message is. . . . Wait.
Are you sure? An echo?
An echo of an echo?
                      Sound.
Was it always there
                with us failing
to hear it?
                What was the shell doing
on the shore? An ear endlessly
              drinking?
            What? Sound? Silence?
Which came first?
                  Listen.
I'll tell you a story
as it was told me by the teller
            of stories.
Where did he hear it?
By listening? To silence? To sound?
        To an echo? To an echo
                          of an echo?
                          Wait.

THE BUSH

I know that bush,
Moses; there are many of them
in Wales in the autumn, braziers
where the imagination
warms itself. I have put off
pride and, knowing the ground

holy, lingered to wonder
how it is that I do not burn
and yet am consumed.

And in this country
of failure, the rain
falling out of a black
cloud in gold pieces there
are none to gather,
I have thought often
of the fountain of my people
that played beautifully here
once in the sun's light
like a tree undressing.

SLEIGHT

As though a voice
        said to me not
in words: I ask the supreme
        gesture. Take me
as I am. And the sky
was round as though everything
was inside.
                But my mind,
I said, holding it
                in my unseen
hands: the pain of it
                is what keeps
me human. What you ask
        is an assemblage
that shall pass unscathed
                through the bonfire
of its knowledge.
                        You do yourself
        harm, coming to us

with your sleeves rolled up
        as though not responsible
for deception. We have seen
you lay life like a cloth
                over the bones
at our parties and wave
        your cold wand and expect
us to smile, when you took it away
        again and there was nothing.

CALLER

On the doorstep
                representing
    the world
full of decency
        because it wants something.
                And I offered
a chance to give,
        do I concentrate
                on the chin's pimple,
on the money he will make,
on the wife's ugliness
                behind him, cumbrous
        as a calf in tow?

I see him as somebody's infant
        once, recipient
        of love's showers pouring
                unwanted.
I see the halo over
                him swelling
        to the nuclear cloud.
Friend, I say,
        nursing him with my eyes
                from the bone's

cancer, since we are at death's
　　door, come in,
let us peer at eternity
through the cracks in each other's hearts.

CONTACTS

The wheel revolves
　　　　to bring round the hour
for this one to return to the darkness
and be born again on a chill
　　　　doorstep, and have the blood washed
from his eyes and his hands
　　　　made clean for the re-building

of the city. While for this one
　　　it revolves to make the tanks
　　　stronger the aeroplanes faster.

The scholar bends over
his book and the sage his navel
　　　to enter the labyrinthine
mind and find at the centre the axis
on which it spins. But for the one
　　　　who is homeless
there is only the tree with the body
　　　on it, eternally convulsed
by the shock of its contact
with the exposed nerve of love.

SELAH!

Listening to history's
babble; not understanding.
Interpreting it even so
for the sake of an audience.

Symphonies raise up
their fiery architecture.
Pages that were once white
carry the poet's rubric.

Man milks his tears
from a venomous tooth;
excuses Eve
under a bi-sexual tree.

The desert annually
thickens its dry tide
under the loaded scapegoat's
too innocent cropping.

INSIDE

I am my own
geology, strata on strata
of the imagination, tufa
dreams, the limestone mind
honeycombed by the running away
of too much thought. Examine
me, tap with your words'
hammer, awaken memories
of fire. It is so long
since I cooled. Inside me,
stalactite and stalagmite,
ideas have formed and become
rigid. To the crowd
I am all outside.
To the pot-holing few there is a way
in along passages that become
narrower and narrower,
that lead to the chamber
too low to stand up in,
where the breath condenses
to the cold and locationless

cloud we call truth. It
is where I think.

ISLAND

Of all things to remember
this is special: the Buddha
seated cross-legged, disproving
Donne, himself an island

surrounded by the expanses
of space and time. From his navel
the tree grows whose canopy
is knowledge. He counts the leaves

as they fall, that are words
out of the mouth of the unseen
God, washing his thoughts clean
in them. Over the waters

he sees the argosies of the world
approaching, that will never
arrive, that will go down, each
one sunk by the weight of its own cargo.

SUDDENLY

Suddenly after long silence
he has become voluble.
He addresses me from a myriad
directions with the fluency
of water, the articulateness
of green leaves; and in the genes,
too, the components
of my existence. The rock,

so long speechless, is the library
of his poetry. He sings to me
in the chain-saw, writes
with the surgeon's hand
on the skin's parchment messages
of healing. The weather
is his mind's turbine
driving the earth's bulk round
and around on its remedial
journey. I have no need
to despair; as at
some second Pentecost
of a Gentile, I listen to the things
round me: weeds, stones, instruments,
the machine itself, all
speaking to me in the vernacular
of the purposes of One who is.

AS THOUGH

As though there were no time
like the present and that
vanishing. As though Sirius were not
light years away and the universe
endlessly old. As though
there were not in the earth's
acres room for a thousand
like him and as many
bosoms, whiter than mine,
for him to lay his head
on. Love me, he said, holding
his two hands out like a beggar
so I could drop my child in them,
one more creature to grow up
in a world that goes tirelessly round,
trying to understand what distances are.

ARRIVAL

Not conscious
  that you have been seeking
      suddenly
  you come upon it

the village in the Welsh hills
      dust free
  with no road out
but the one you came in by.

      A bird chimes
  from a green tree
the hour that is no hour
  you know. The river dawdles
to hold a mirror for you
where you may see yourself
  as you are, a traveller
      with the moon's halo
  above him, who has arrived
  after long journeying where he
      began, catching this
  one truth by surprise
that there is everything to look forward to.

BROTHER

It came into being.
From eternity? In
time? Was the womb
prepared for it, or it
for the womb? It lay in the cradle
long months, staring its world
into a shape, decorated
with faces. It addressed
objects, preferred its vocabulary

to their own; grew eloquent
before a resigned
audience. It was fed
speech and vomited
it and was not reproved.
It began walking,
falling, bruising itself
on the bone's truth. The fire
was a tart playmate. It
was taken in by the pool's smile.
Need I go on? It survived
its disasters; met fact
with the mind's guile; forged
for itself wings, missiles.
Launched itself on a dark
night through the nursery
window into adult orbit
out of the reach of gravity's control.

REMEMBERING DAVID JONES

Because you had been in the dark wood
and heard doom's nightingales sing,
men listened to you when you told
them how death is many but life
one. The shell's trumpet sounded
over the fallen, but there was no
resurrection. You learned your lettering
from bones, the propped capitals which described
how once they were human beings.

Men march because they are alive,
and their quest is the Grail, garrisoned
by the old furies so it is blood
wets their lips. Europe gave you
your words, but your hand practised

an earlier language, weaving time's branches
together to form the thicket the soldier
is caught in, who is love's sacrifice
to itself, with the virgin's smile poised
like a knive over it as over her first born.

THE MOMENT

Is the night dark? His interiors
are darker, more perilous
to enter. Are there whispers
abroad? They are the communing

with himself our destiny
is to be outside of, listeners
at our breath's window. Is there
an ingredient in him of unlove?

It is the moment in the mind's
garden he resigns himself
to his own will to conceive the tree
of manhood we have reared against him.

GOSPEL

And in the midst of the council
a bittern called from the fen
outside. A sparrow flew in
and disappeared through the far doorway
'If your faith can explain. . . .' So
they were baptised, and the battles began
for the kingdom of this world. Were
you sent, sparrow? An eagle
would have been more appropriate,
some predator to warn them

of the ferocity of the religion
that came their way. The fire was not more voluble
than the blood that would answer the sword's
question.
Charles by divine right
king. And not all our engines can drain
Marston Moor. The bittern is
silent now. The ploughshares are beaten
to guns and bombs. Daily we publish
hurrying with it to and fro on steel
wings, the good news of the kingdom.

ASIDES

Between the closing of an eye
and its opening centuries
of bone cold, a millenium of them.
Beneath all that monumental
ice what art epochs, what religion?
Are those eye-lashes rigid
with tears of possible compassion,
icicles fringing the resigned lids?

The anthropomorphisms of time!
The lineaments he might have confessed
to are elsewhere. What has ubiquity
to do with form? Ah, planetary truth,
inexorable in teaching everything that can be taught
but our mirrors their manners.

CITIZEN

Here for a while heard
voices powerless

to obey looked fear
in the face was outstared
by it took lust
for love burned more
than his fingers saw need
lie dropped it a tear
passed on. Visitors
from a far country
beauty addressed him
truth too he was no
linguist keeping his balance
without grace took
one step forward and one
back on the shining tightrope
between dark and dark.

CAROL

What is Christmas without
snow? We need it
as bread of a cold
climate, ermine to trim

our sins with, a brief
sleeve for charity's
scarecrow to wear its heart
on, bold as a robin.

REQUIEM

To the mature itch I lent my hand;
a sword grew in it, withered
in the exact blood. When next I looked,
murder; the sour commons

attainted me. But the king's head
lapping at the emptying trough
of existence, reprieved me. I took aim
with the long musket, writing in lead
on their horses. Hysterical women
my loot, I rendered complete
service, sowing the blank field again.
Alleluia! The canonade of the bells
rang. I built a cathedral—
to whom? Decorated it with the stone
population, the dumb mouths, the eyes blinded
by distance. Naughtiness of the chisel
in time's hand distorted the features
of those who had looked on that far
face and lived to bear witness.

MINUET

But not to concentrate
on disaster, there are the small
weeds with the caterpillar
at their base that is life's proof
that the beautiful is born
from the demolition of the material.

The butterfly has no
clock. It is always noon
where it is, the sun overhead,
the flower feeding on what feeds
on itself. The wings turn and are sails
of a slow windmill, not to grind
but to be the signal for another
aviator to arrive that the air
may have dancing, a movement
of wings in an invisible
ballroom to a music that,

unheard by ourselves, is to them
as though it will never cease.

SONATA

Evening. The wind rising.
The gathering excitement
of the leaves, and Beethoven
on the piano, chords reverberating
in our twin being.
                    'What is life?'
pitifully her eyes asked. And I who was no seer
took hold of her loth hand
and examined it and was lost
like a pure mathematician
in its solution: strokes
cancelling strokes; angles
bisected; the line of life deviating
from the line of the head; a way
that was laid down for her to walk
which was not my way.
                      While the music
went on and on with chromatic
insistence, passionately proclaiming
by the keys' moonlight in the darkening
drawing-room how our art is our meaning.

PRAYER

Baudelaire's grave
not too far
from the tree of science.
Mine, too,
since I sought and failed

to steal from it,
somewhere within sight
of the tree of poetry
that is eternity wearing
the green leaves of time.

INDEX